I0489256

Banana Peel Garden
2014

Banana Peel Garden
Michaela Chapman

Copyright © 2014 Michaela Chapman and Fossil Press.
All rights reserved.

No part of this book may be reproduced in any form or by any
mechanical or electronic means without written permission of the
author, except in the case of brief quotations embodied in critical articles
and reviews.

Published by
Fossil Press
100 Parkwood Avenue
Rochester, New York 14620

Banana Peel Garden is my way of giving back to the world and providing nature with the remnants of its loins: discarded pieces of fruit. What started in the grass outside the window of my first apartment in Rochester, NY, the original Banana Peel Garden, has begun to spread to wherever I travel. I'm planting new seeds, like a modern day Johnny Appleseed, promoting growth in nature through fruit. These photographs are the beginnings of my contributions and findings.

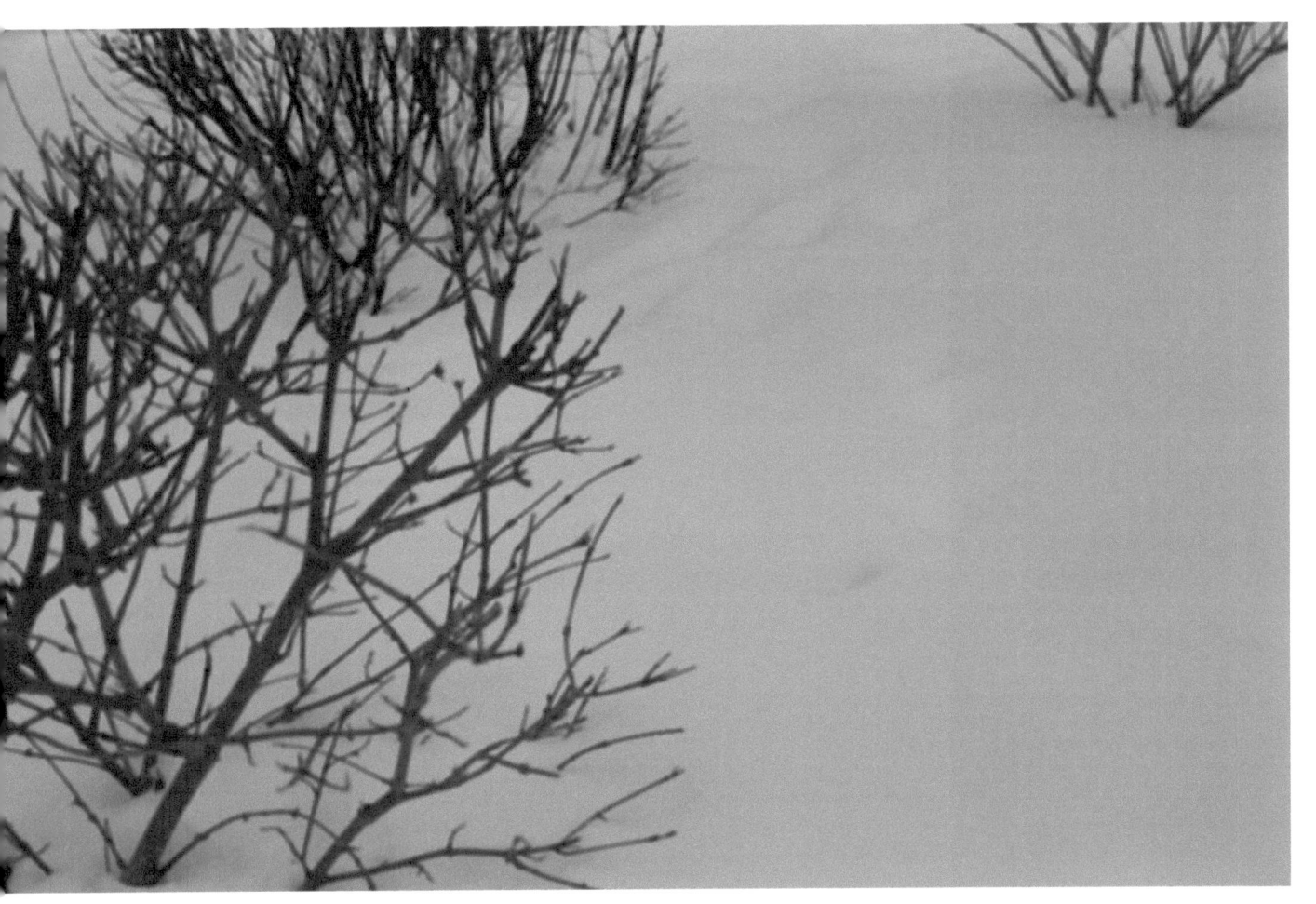

#1 2/13/14 8:40 am Rochester, NY

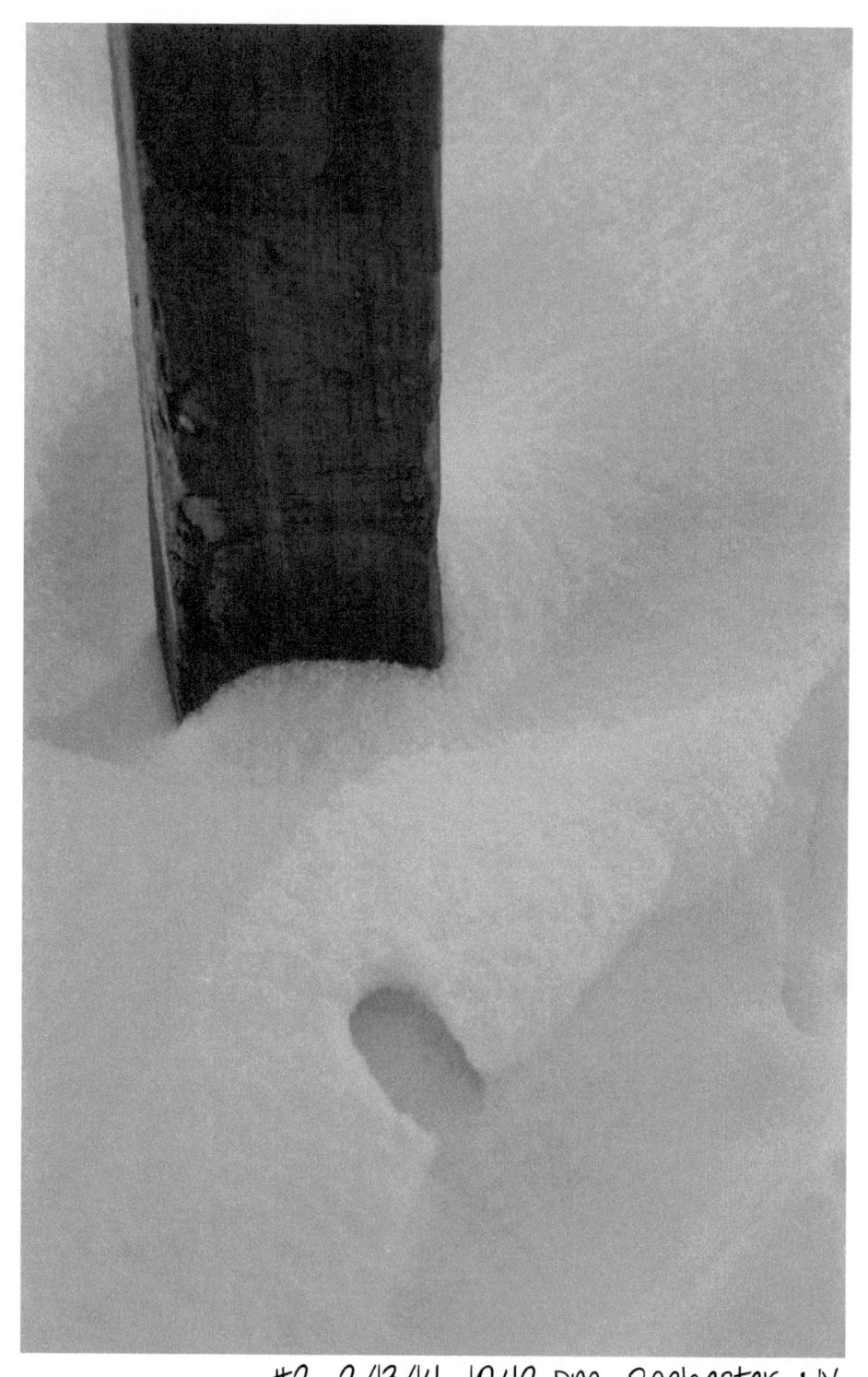

#2 2/13/14 10:42 pm Rochester, NY

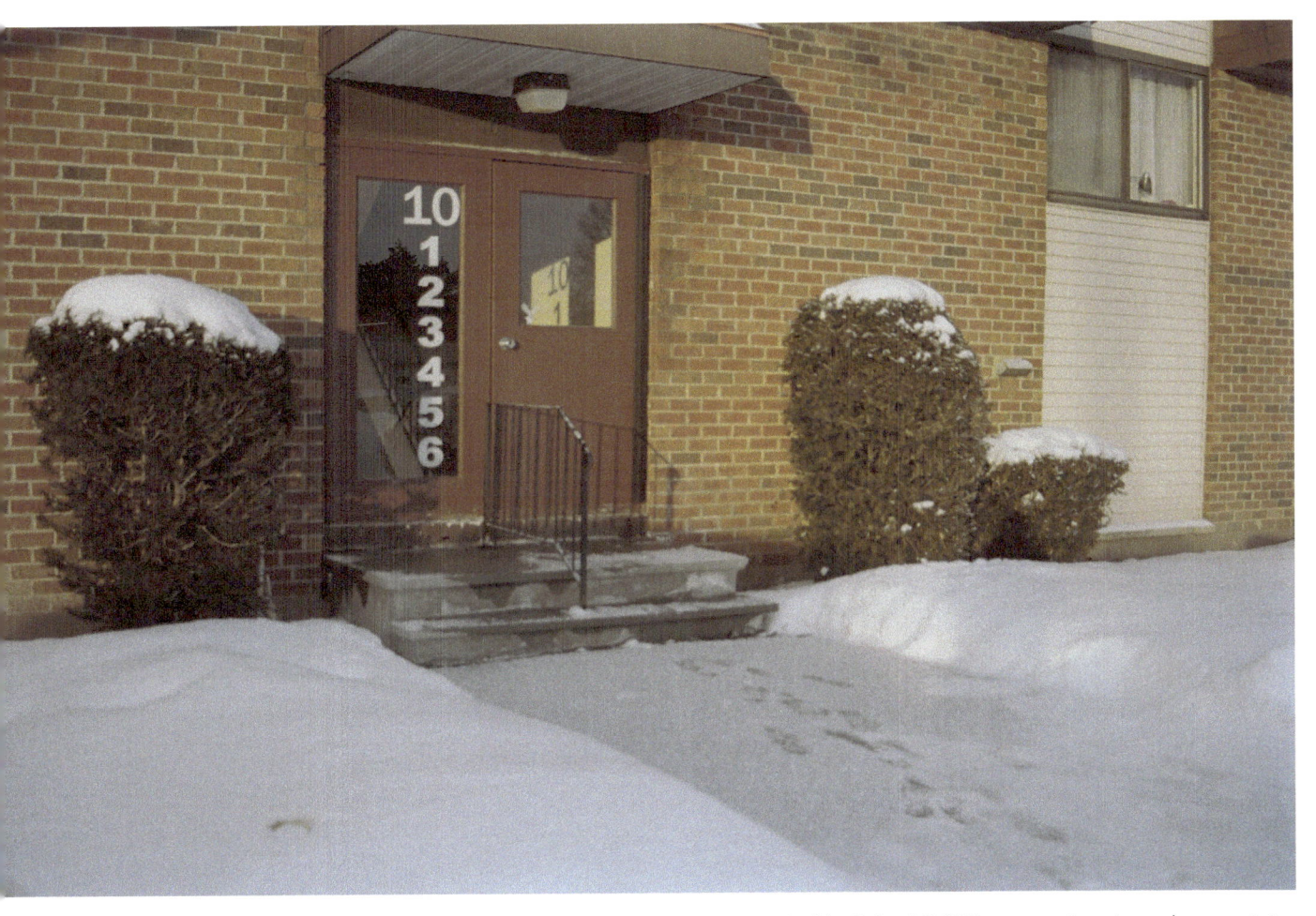

#3 2/16/14 5:05 pm Rochester, NY

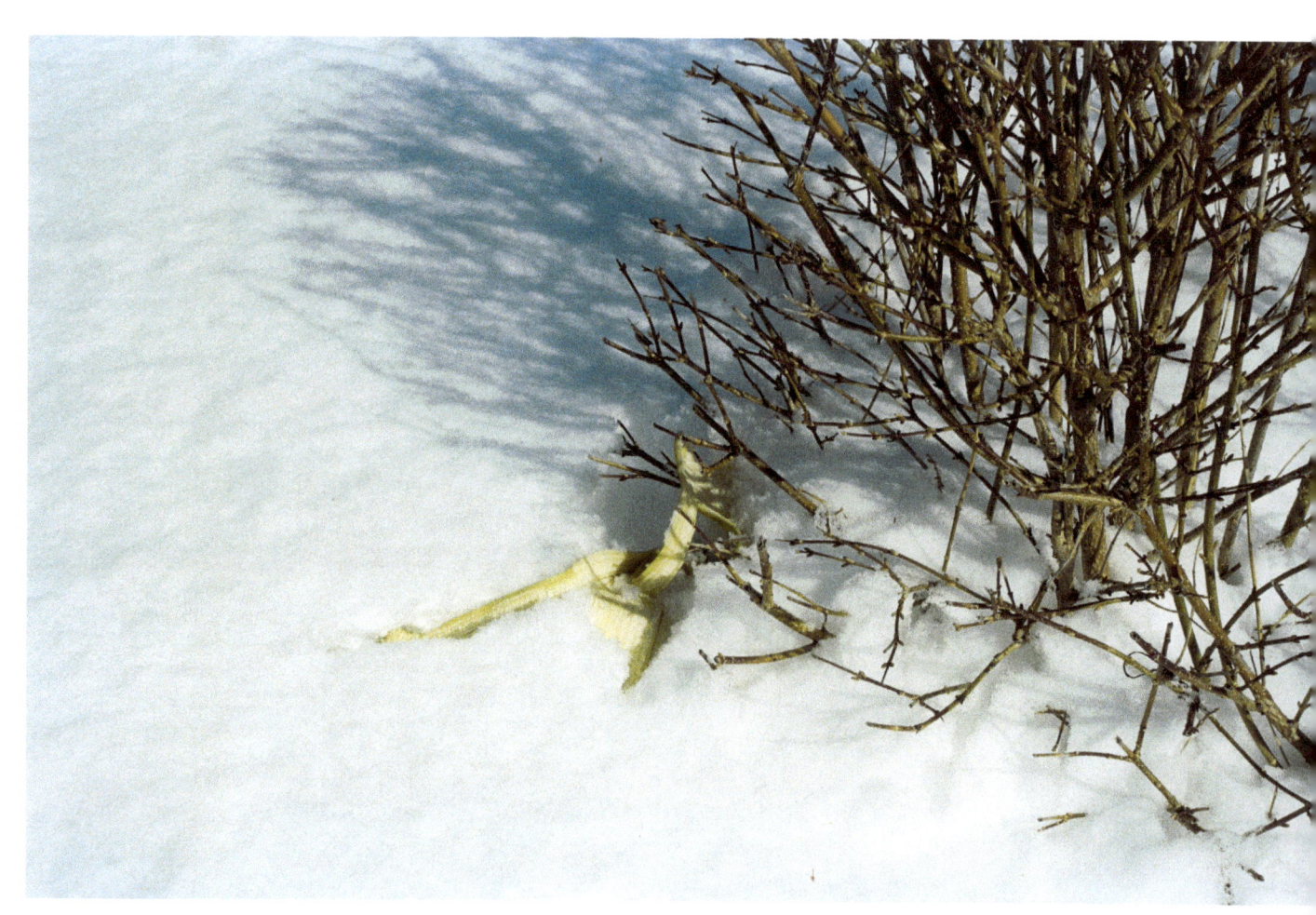

#4 2/17/14 1:33 pm Rochester, NY

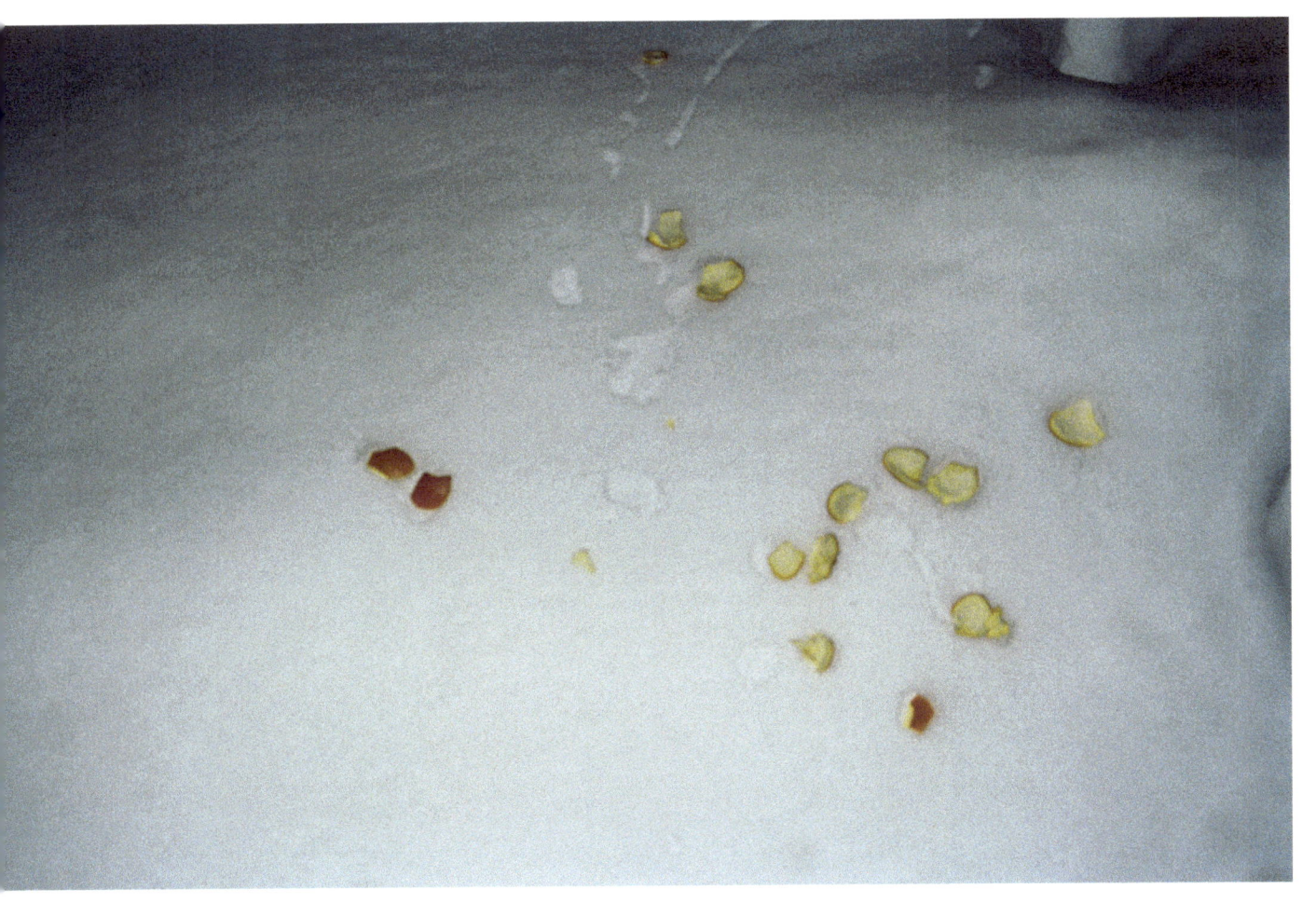

#5 2/17/14 7:00 pm Rochester, NY

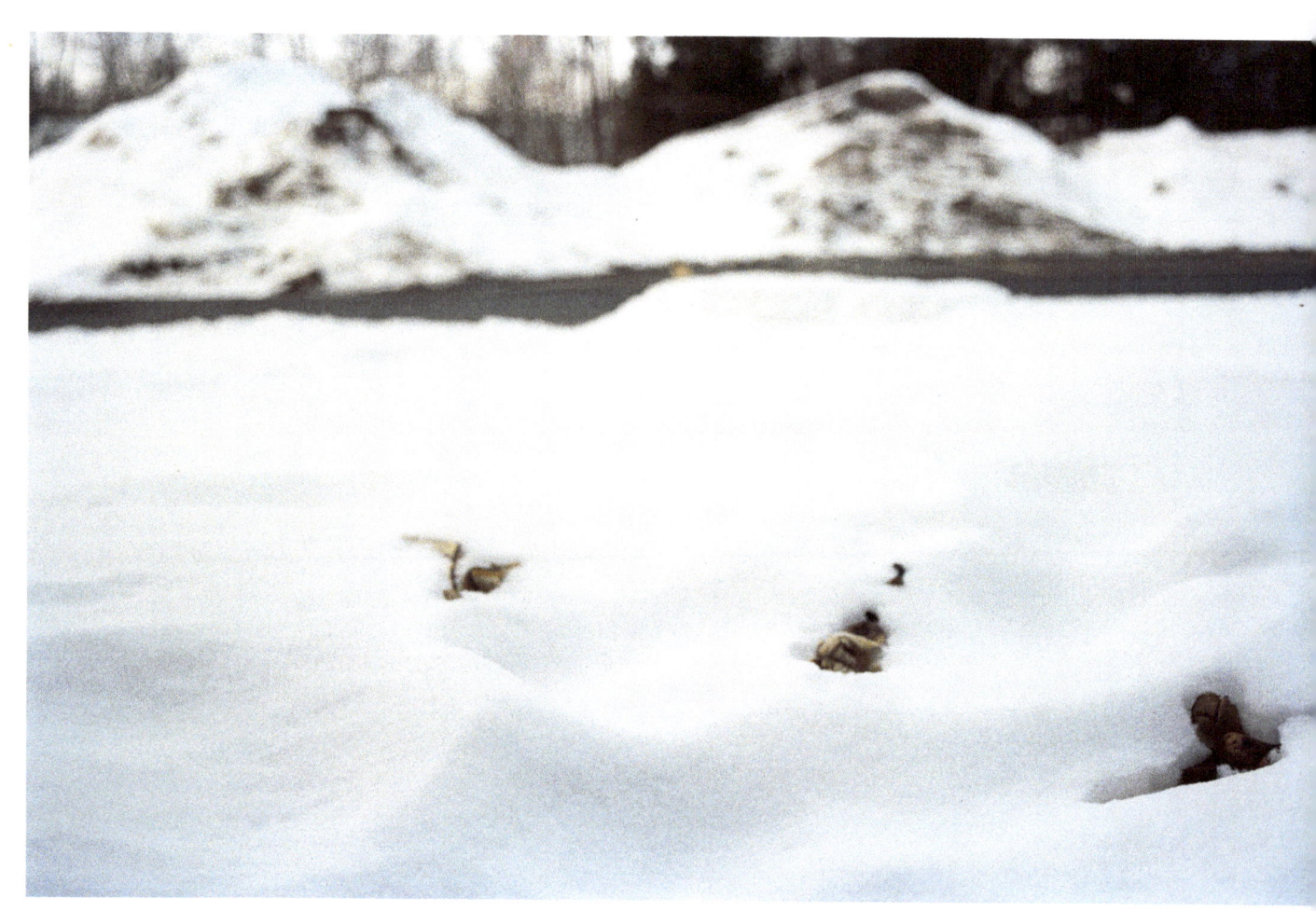

#6 2/18/14 5:20 pm Rochester, NY

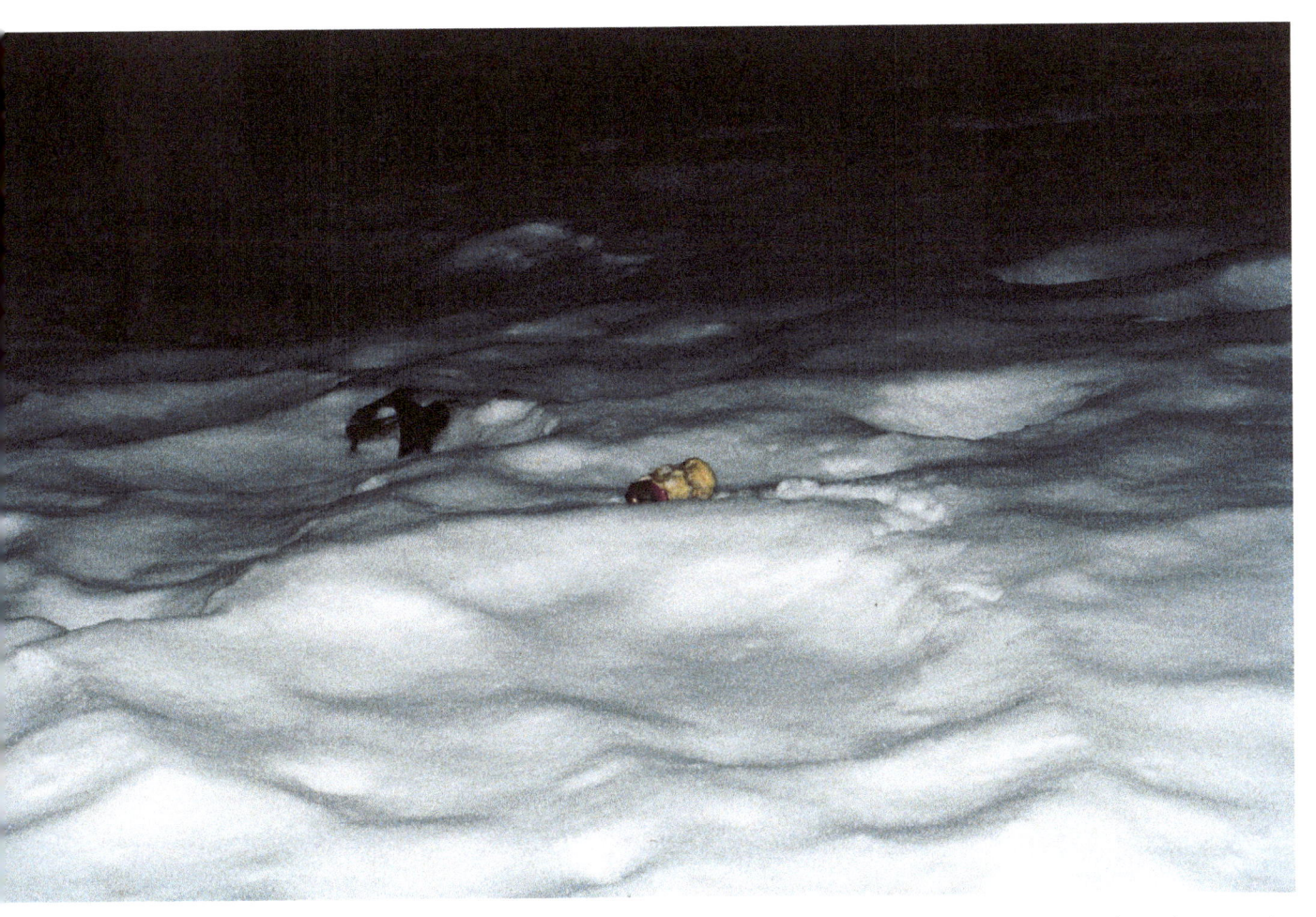

#7 2/25/14 7:26 pm Rochester, NY

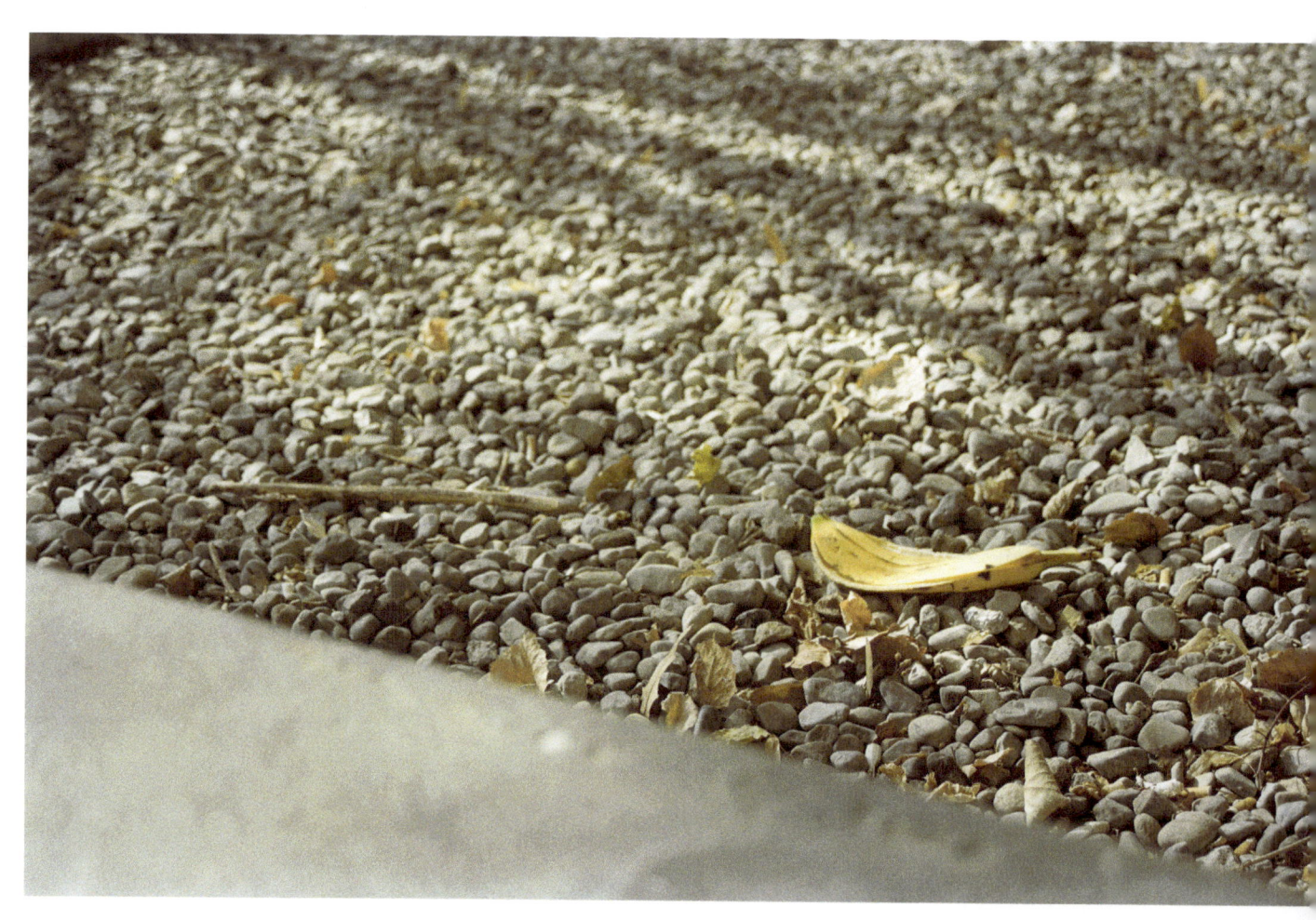

#8 2/26/14 12:53 pm Rochester, NY

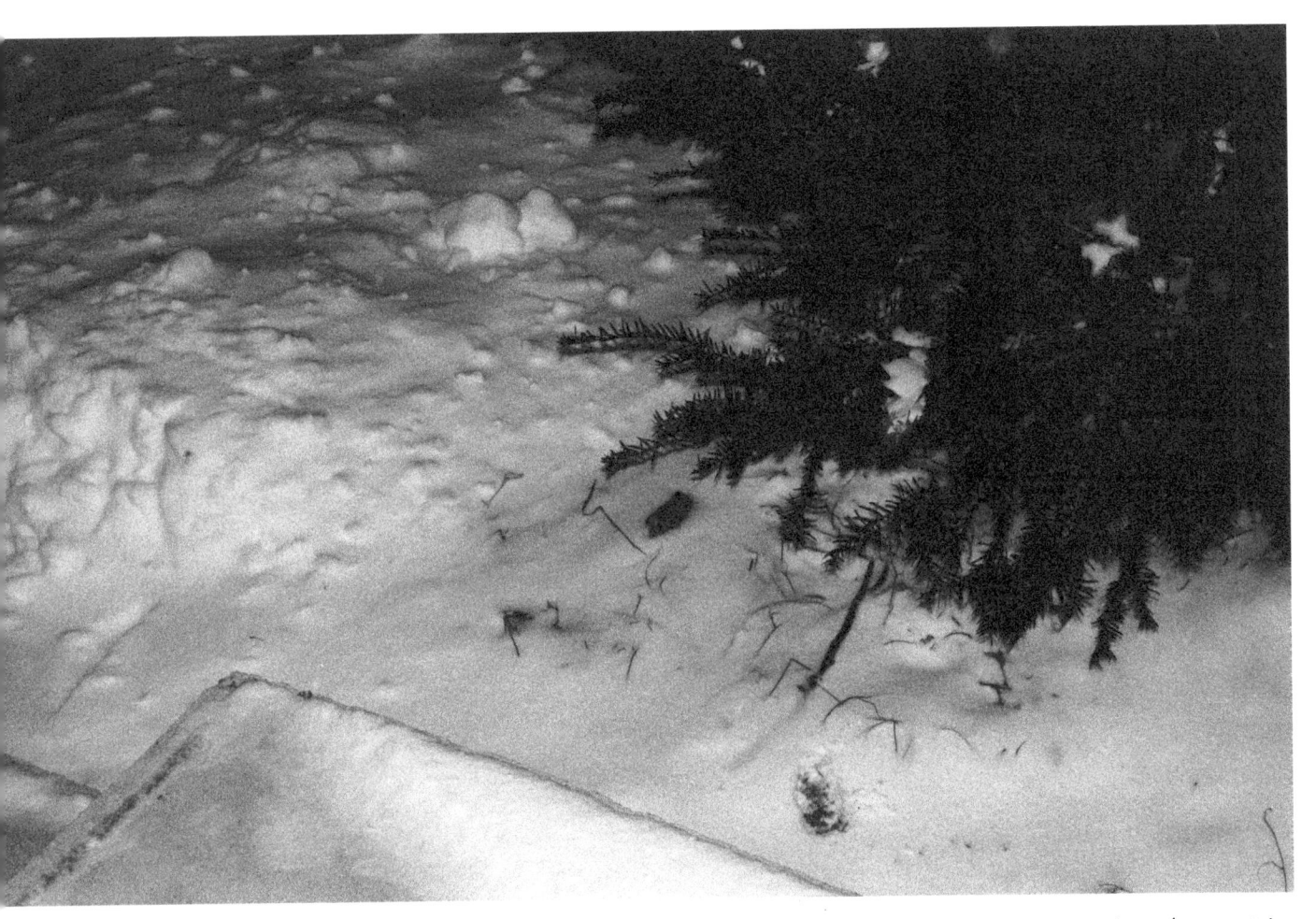

#9 2/28/14 1:05 am Rochester, NY

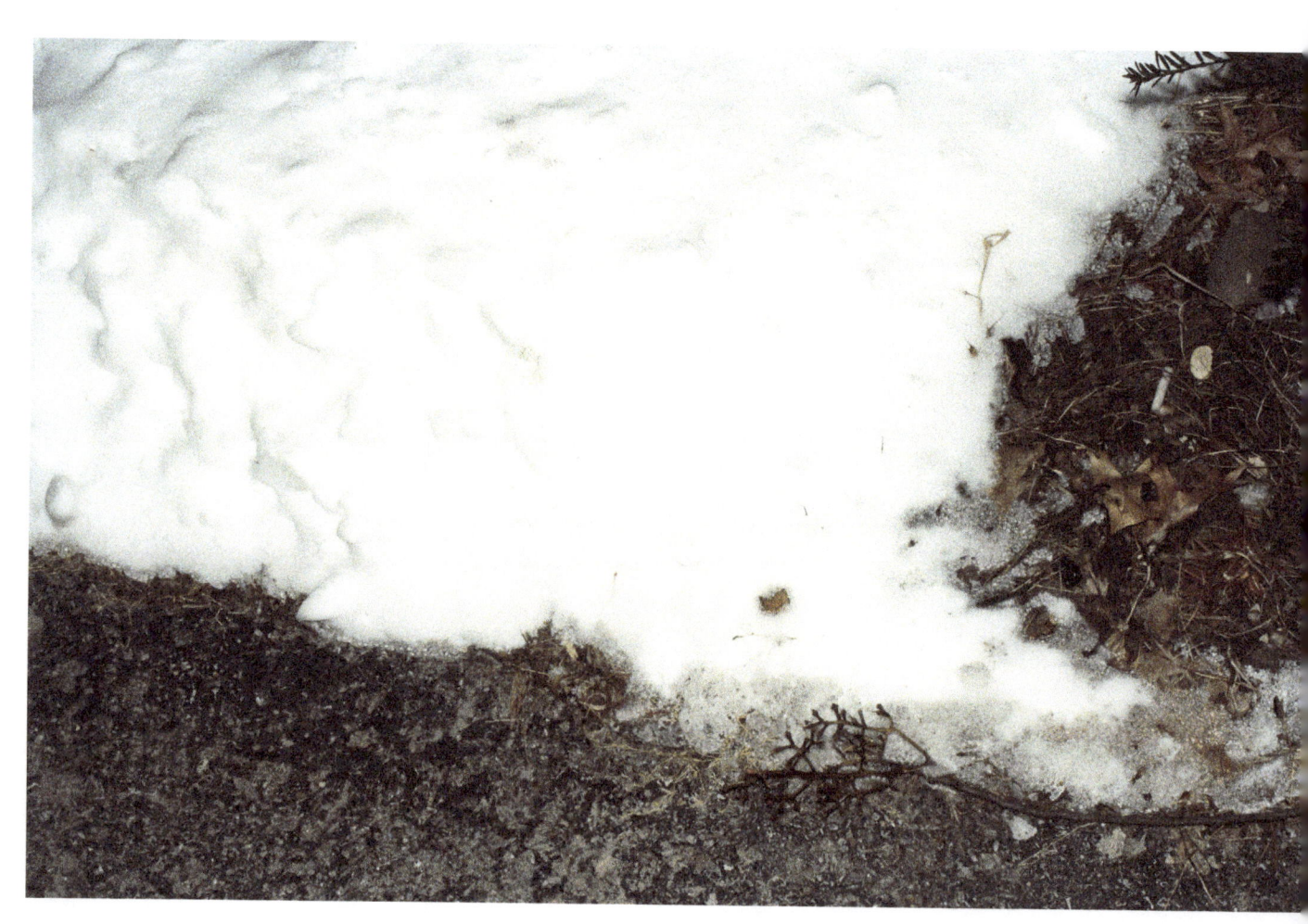

#10 2/28/14 11:23 pm Rochester, NY

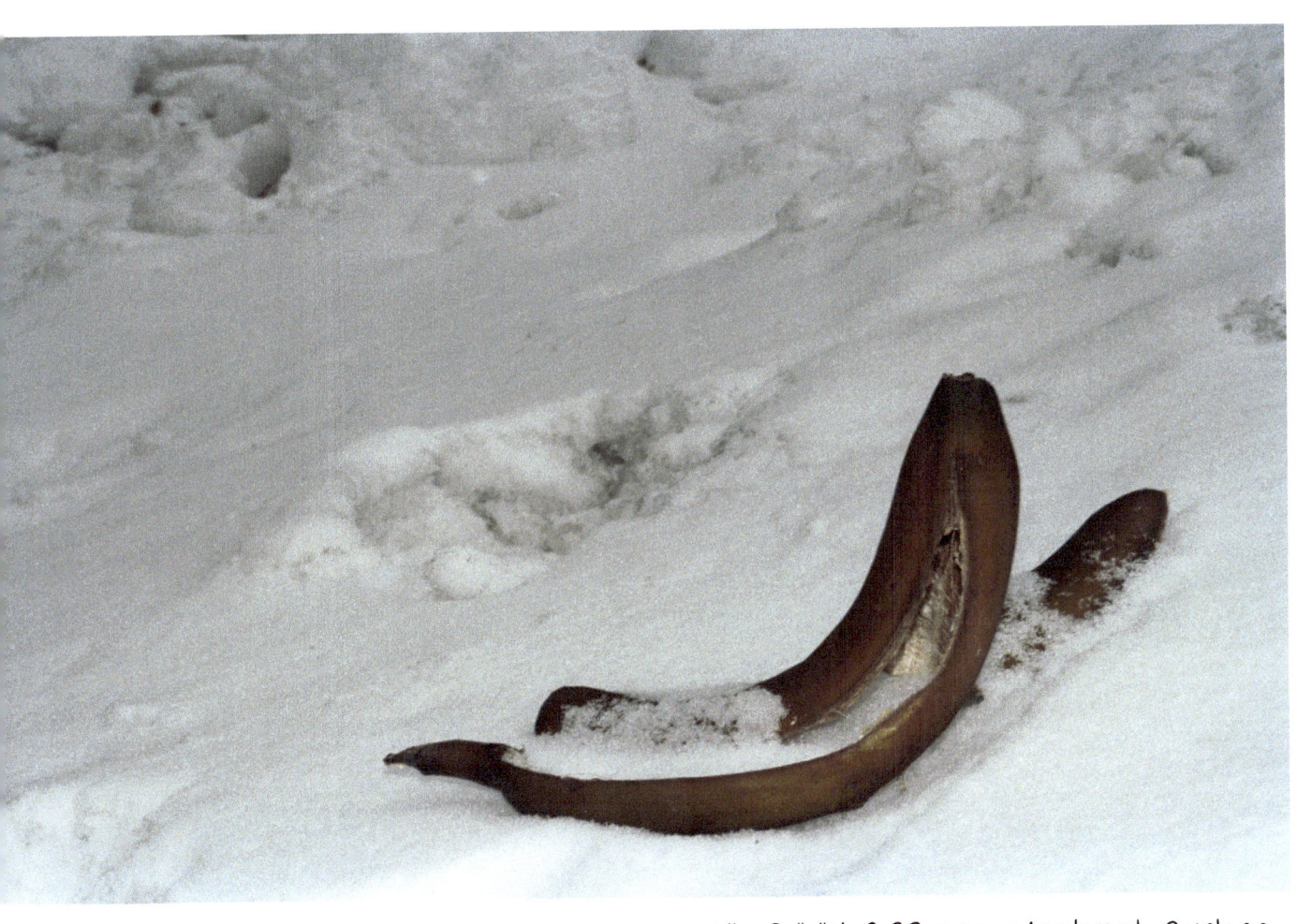

#11 3/1/14 2:33 pm Montreal, Quebec

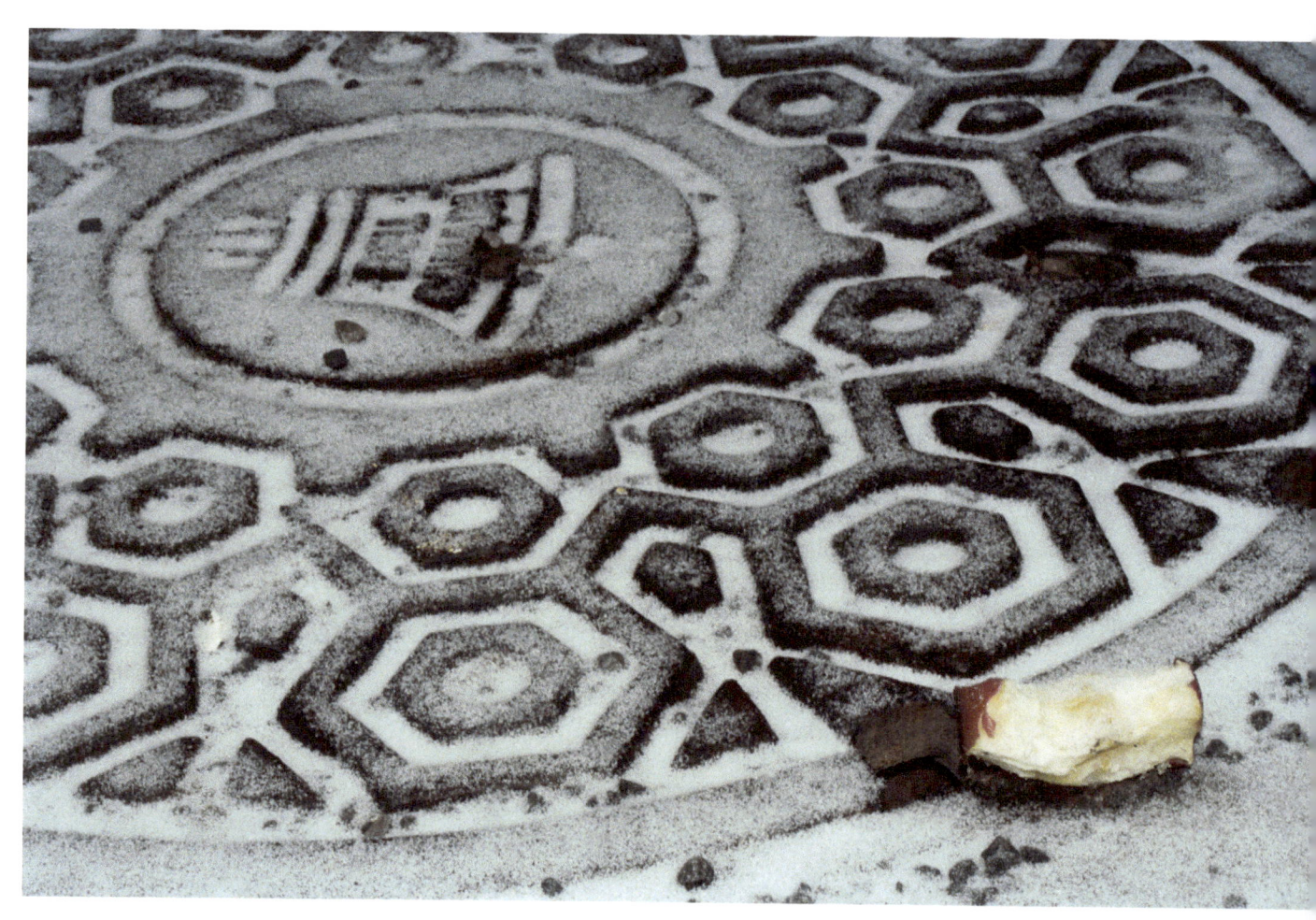

#12 3/1/14 4:04 pm Montreal, Quebec

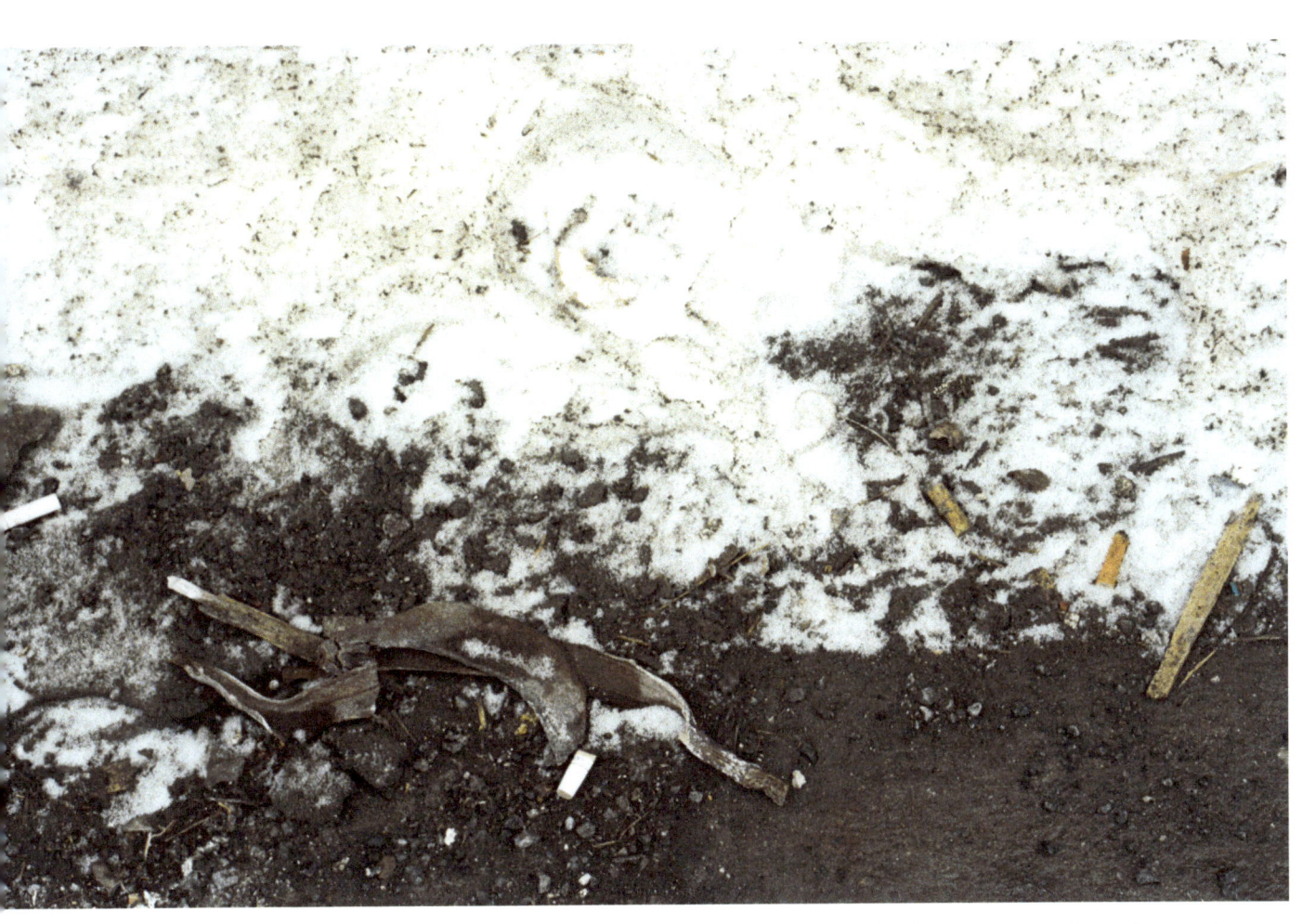

#13 3/1/14 5:27 pm Montreal, Quebec

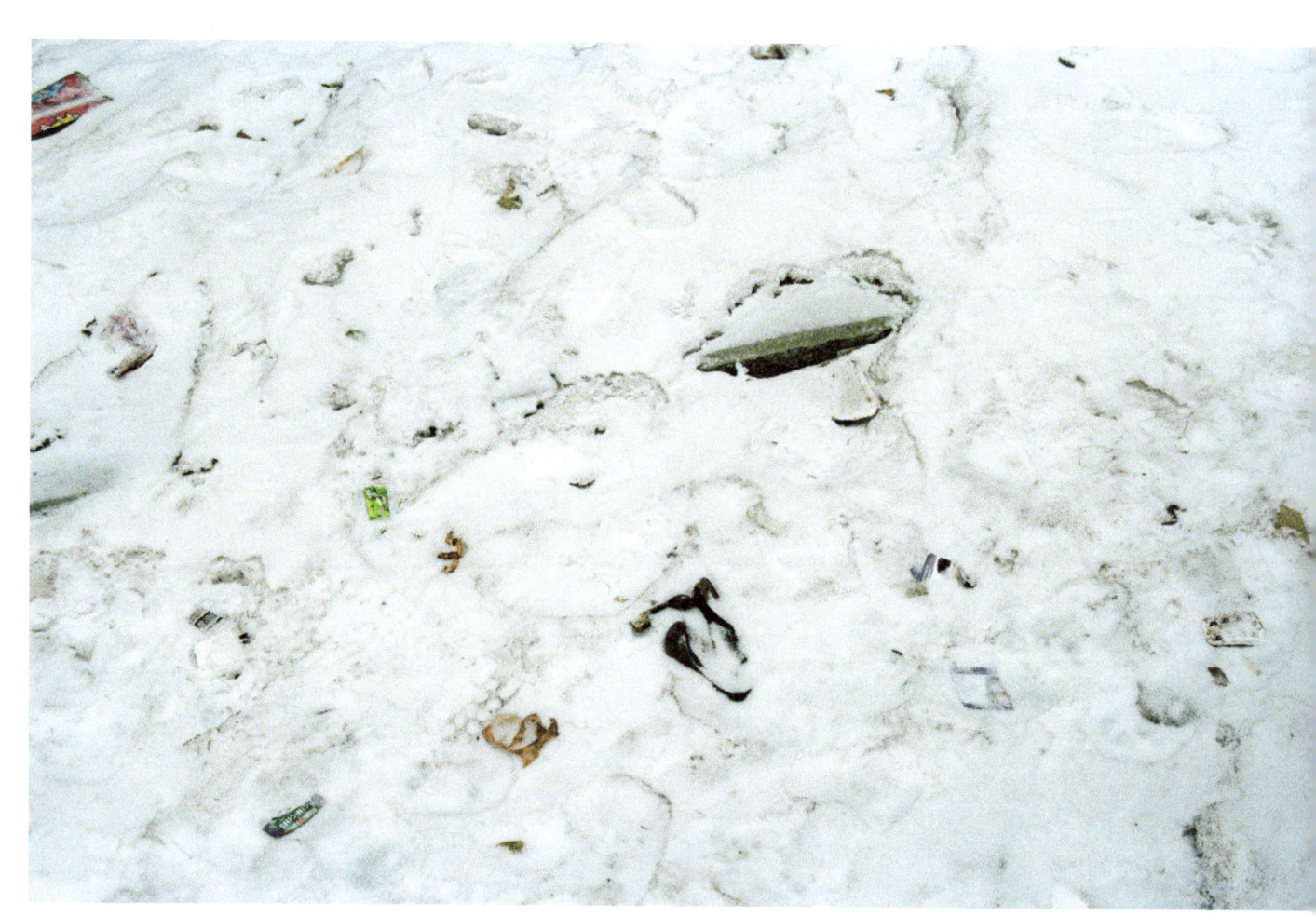

#14 3/1/14 5:30 pm Montreal, Quebec

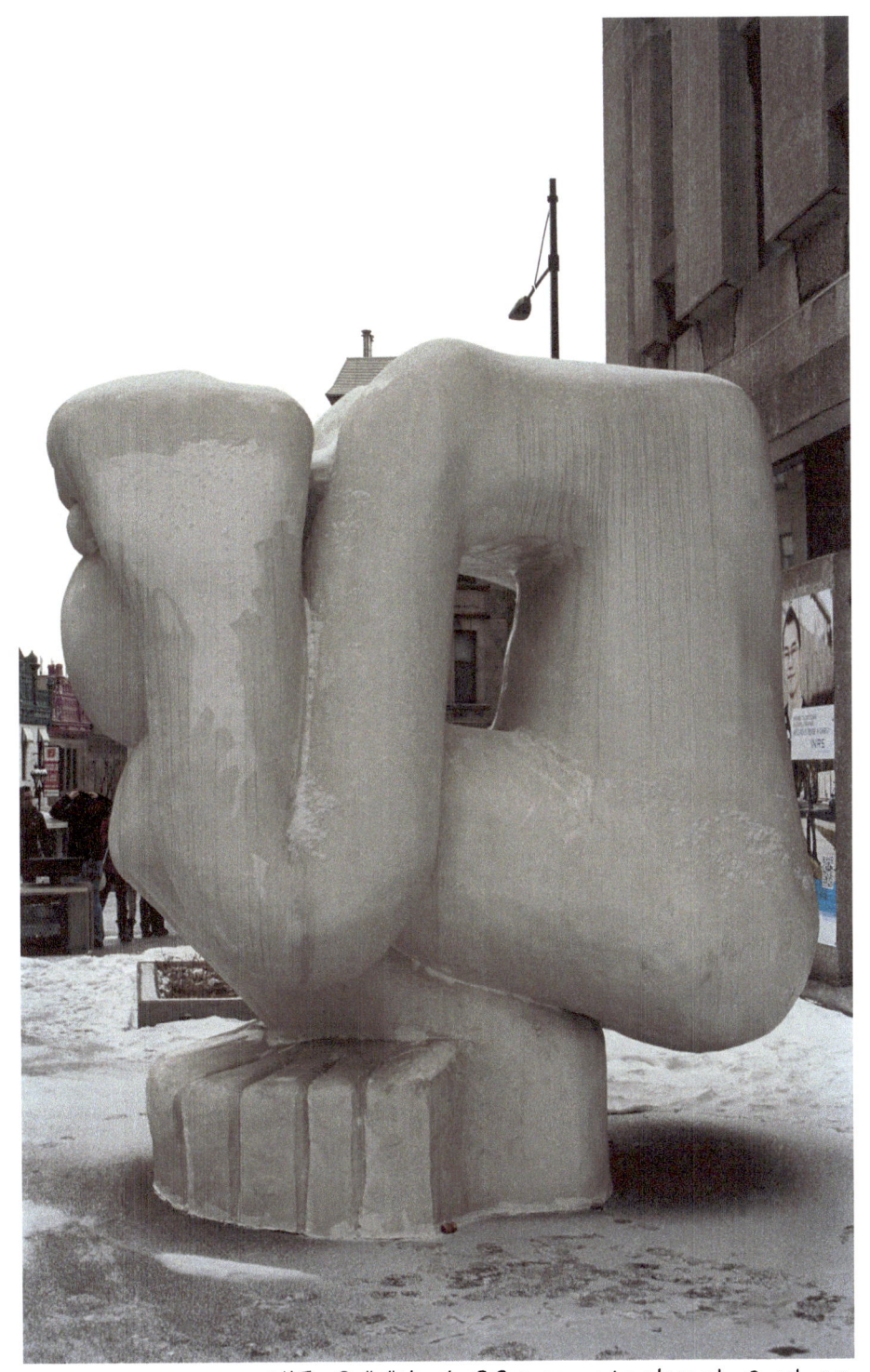

#15 3/1/14 6:09 pm Montreal, Quebec

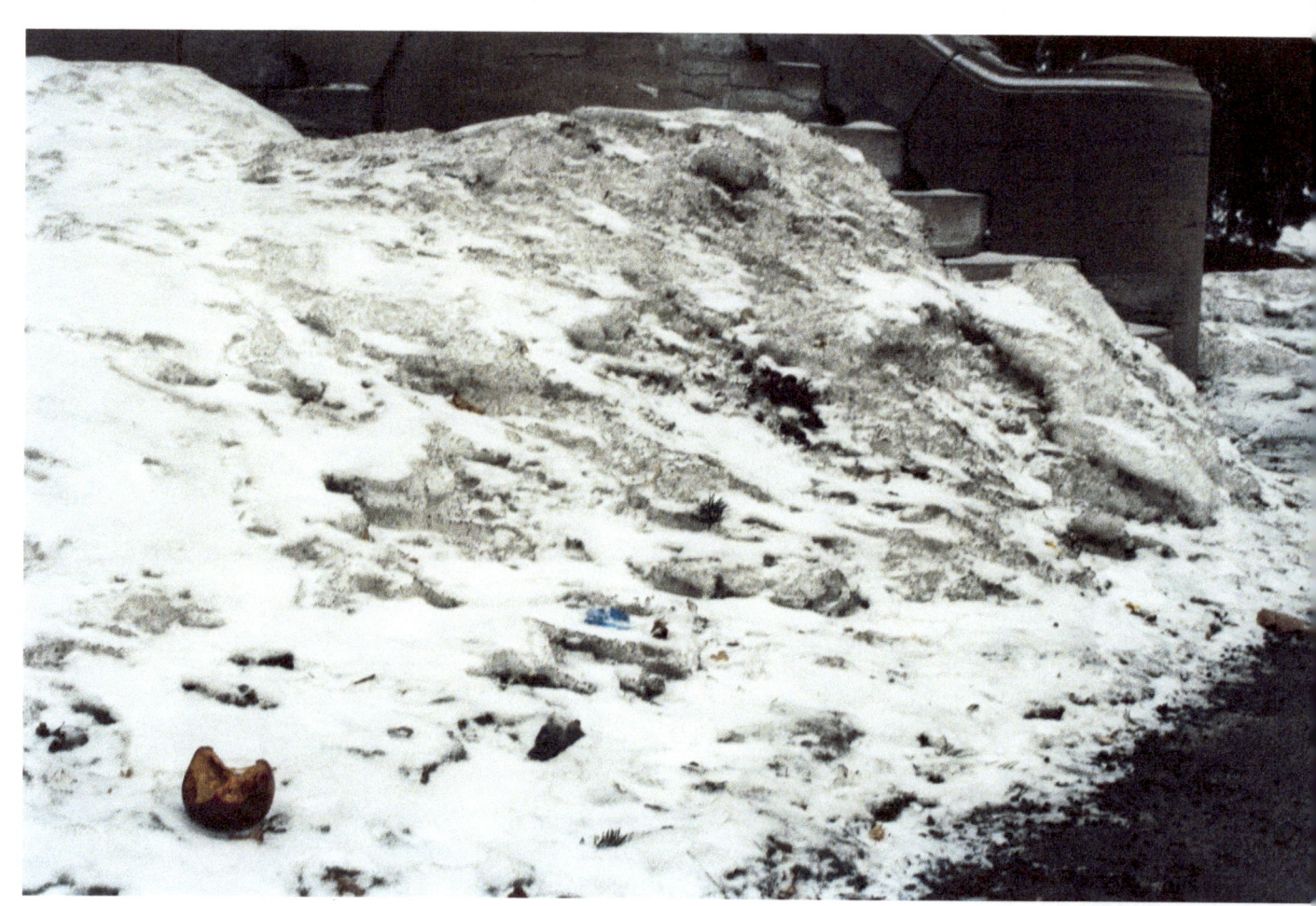

#16 3/1/14 6:23 pm Montreal, Quebec

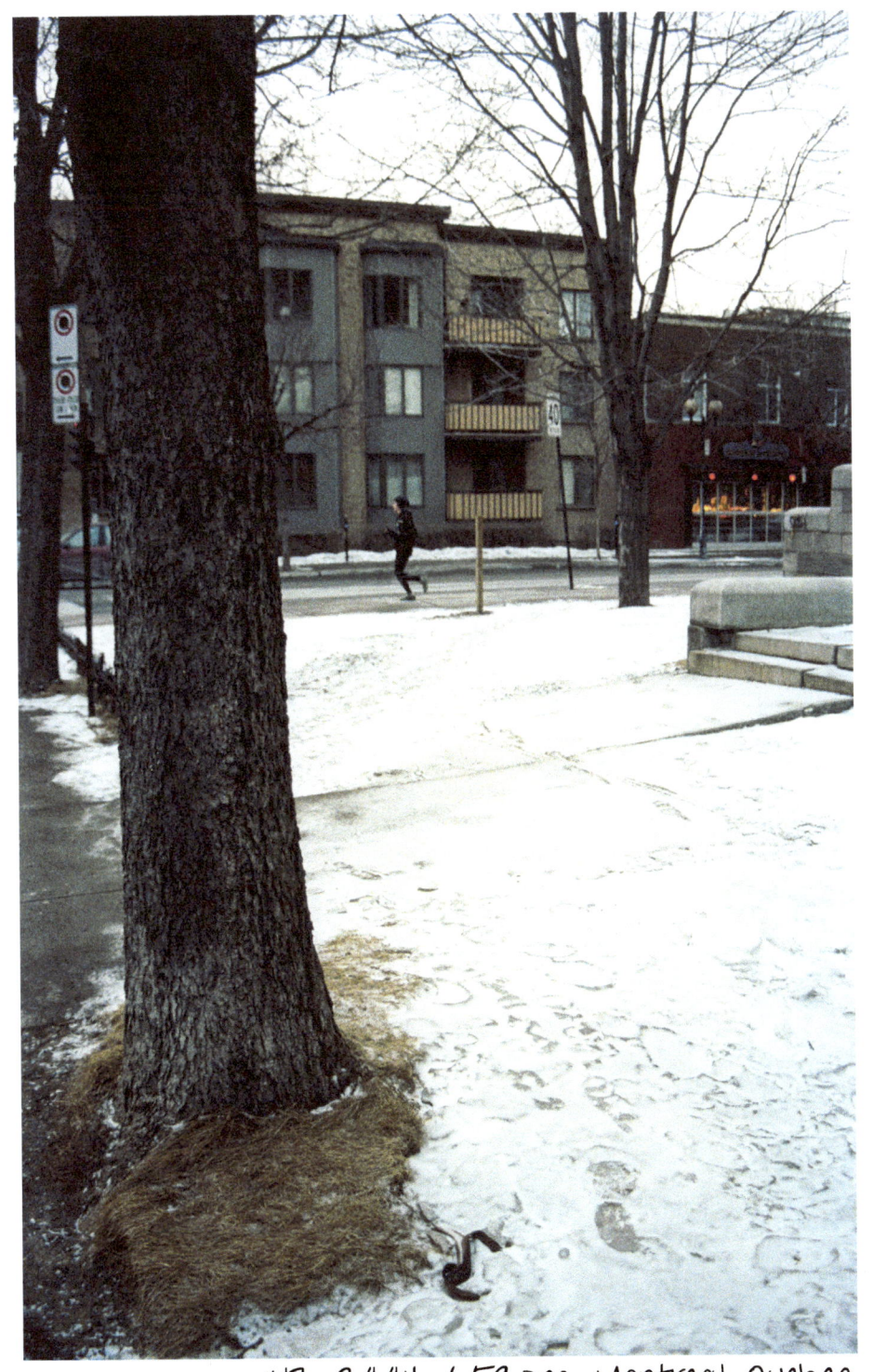

#17 3/1/14 6:59 pm Montreal, Quebec

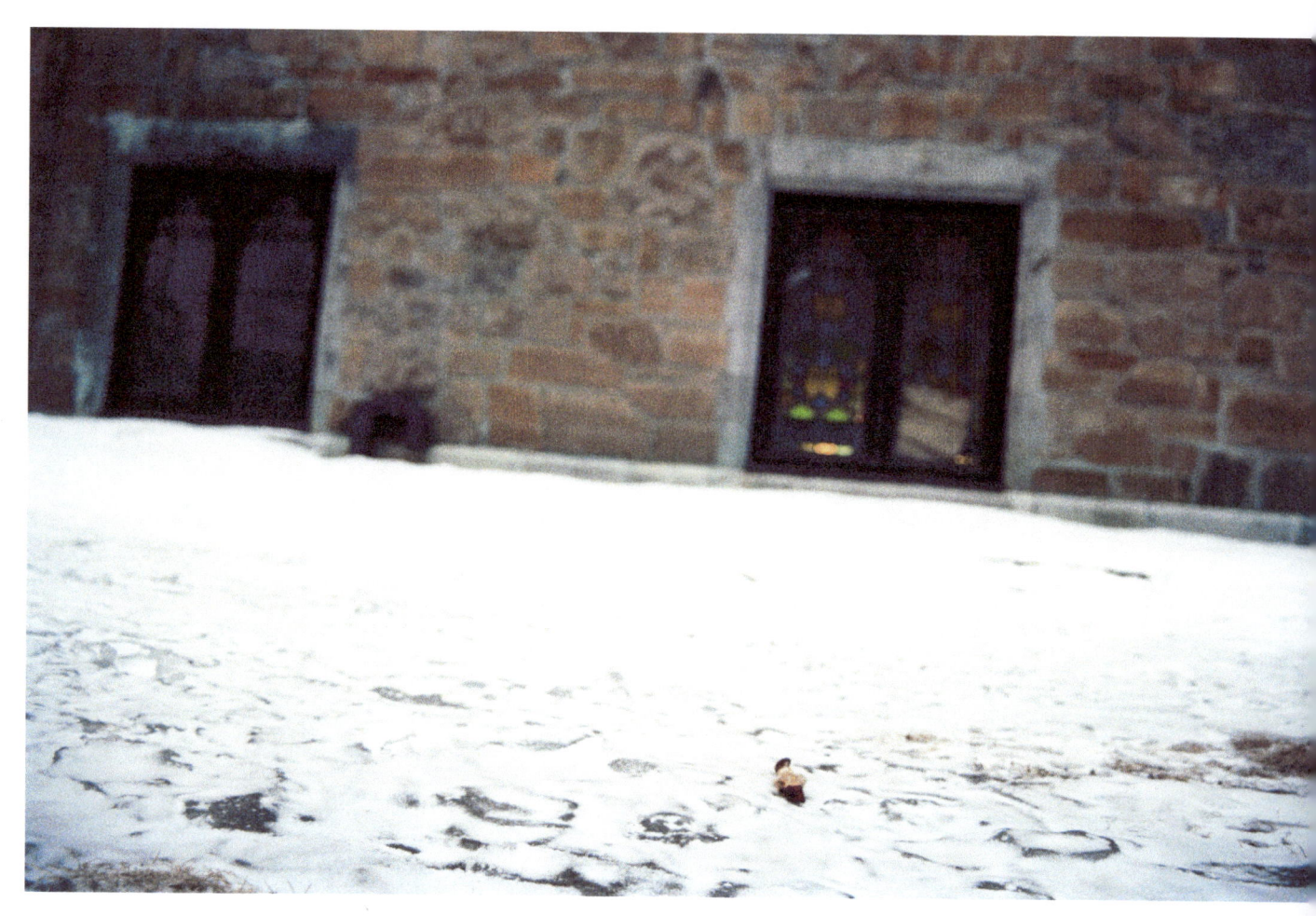

#18 3/1/14 7:44 pm Montreal, Quebec

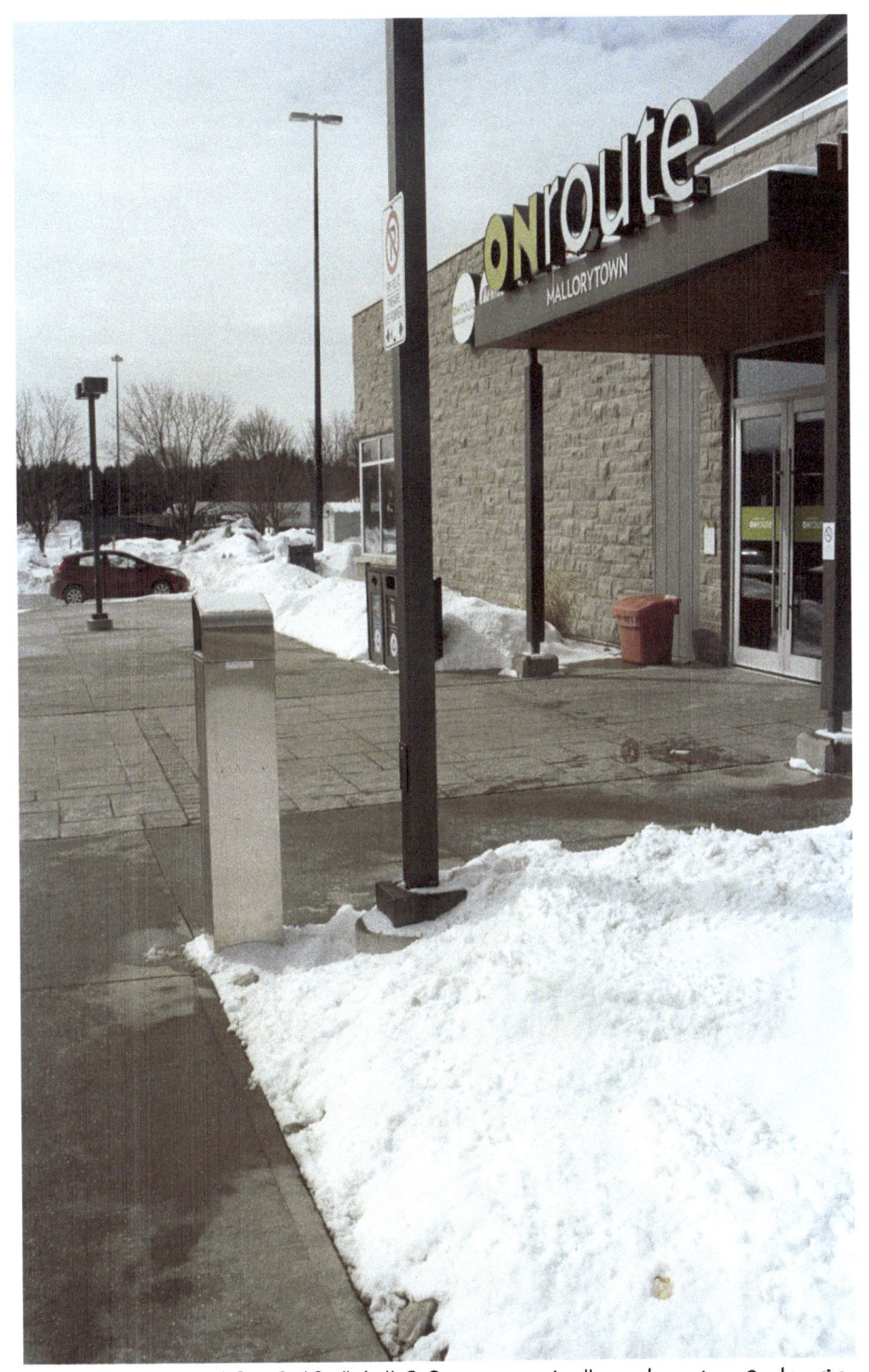

#19 3/2/14 11:30 am Mallorytown, Ontario

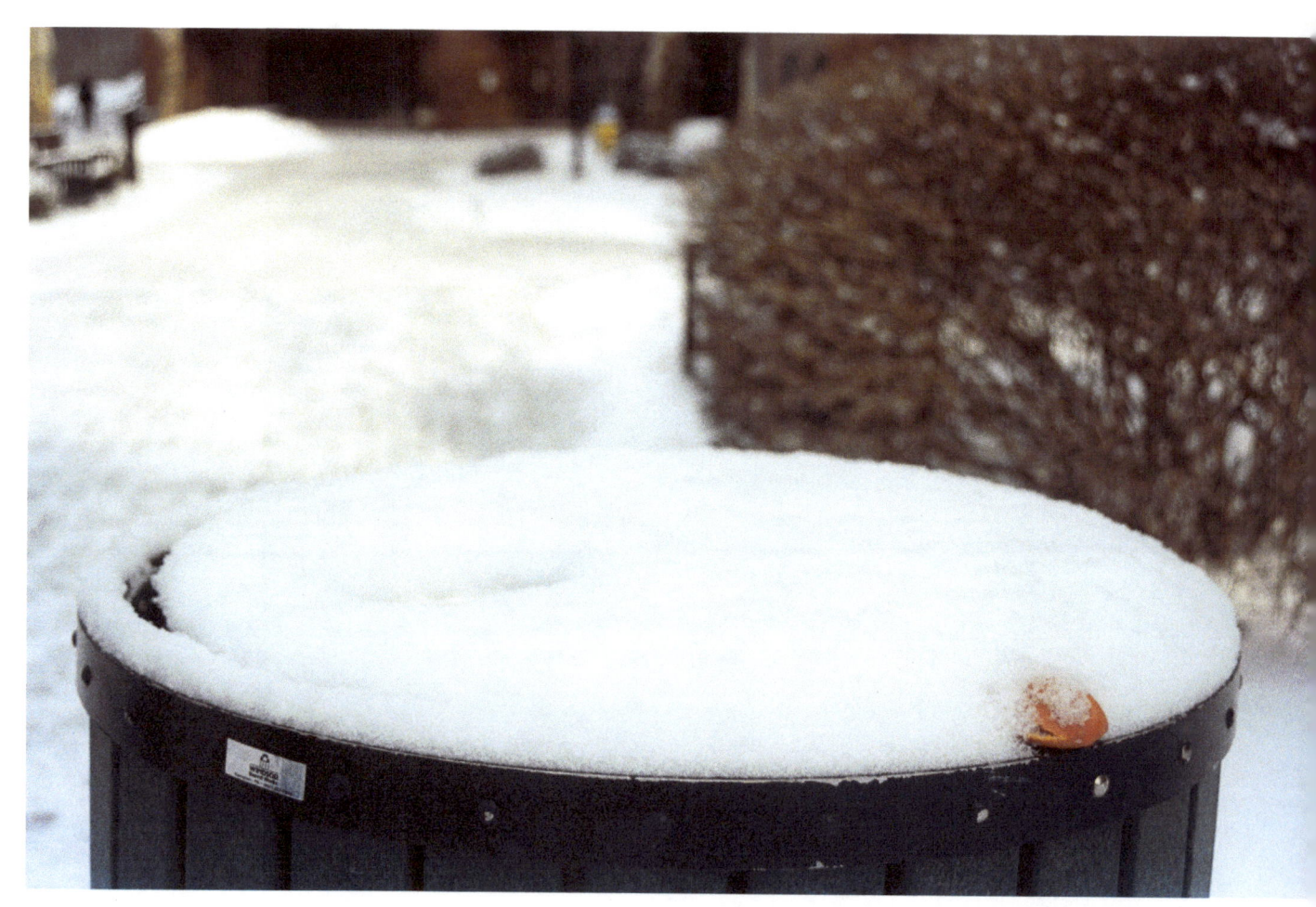

#20 3/5/14 8:44 am Rochester, NY

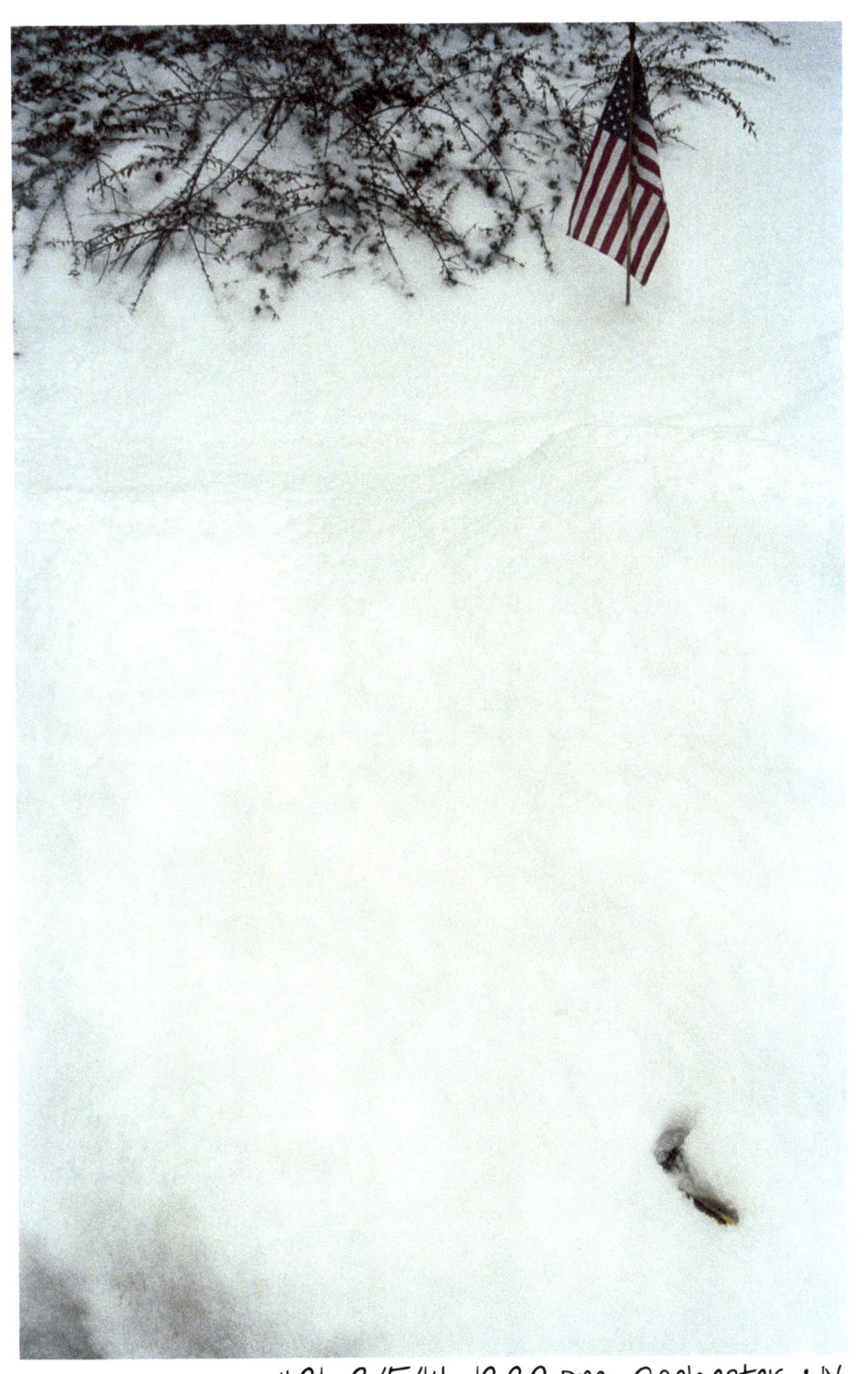

#21 3/5/14 12:20 pm Rochester, NY

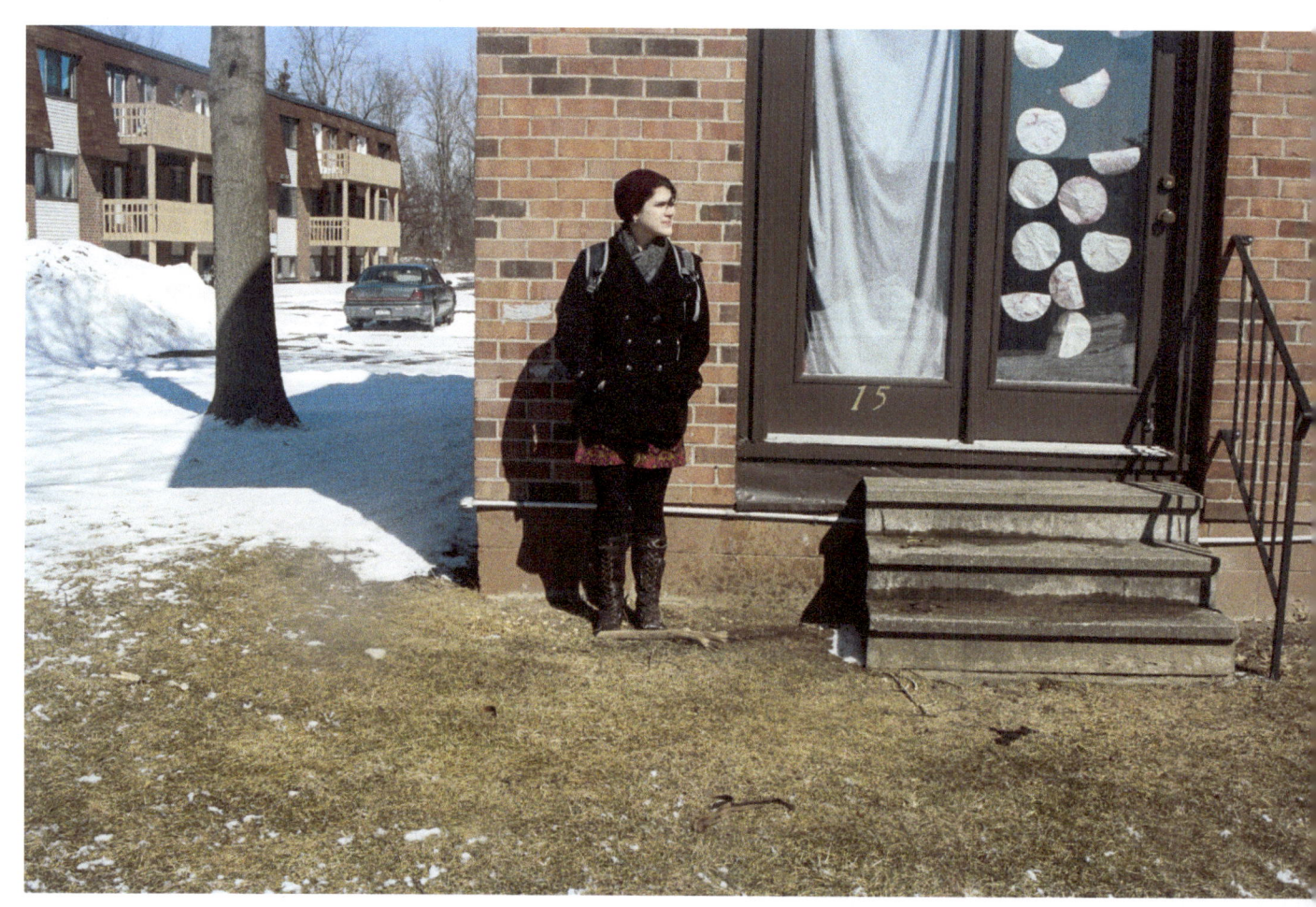

#22 3/6/14 11:57 am Rochester, NY

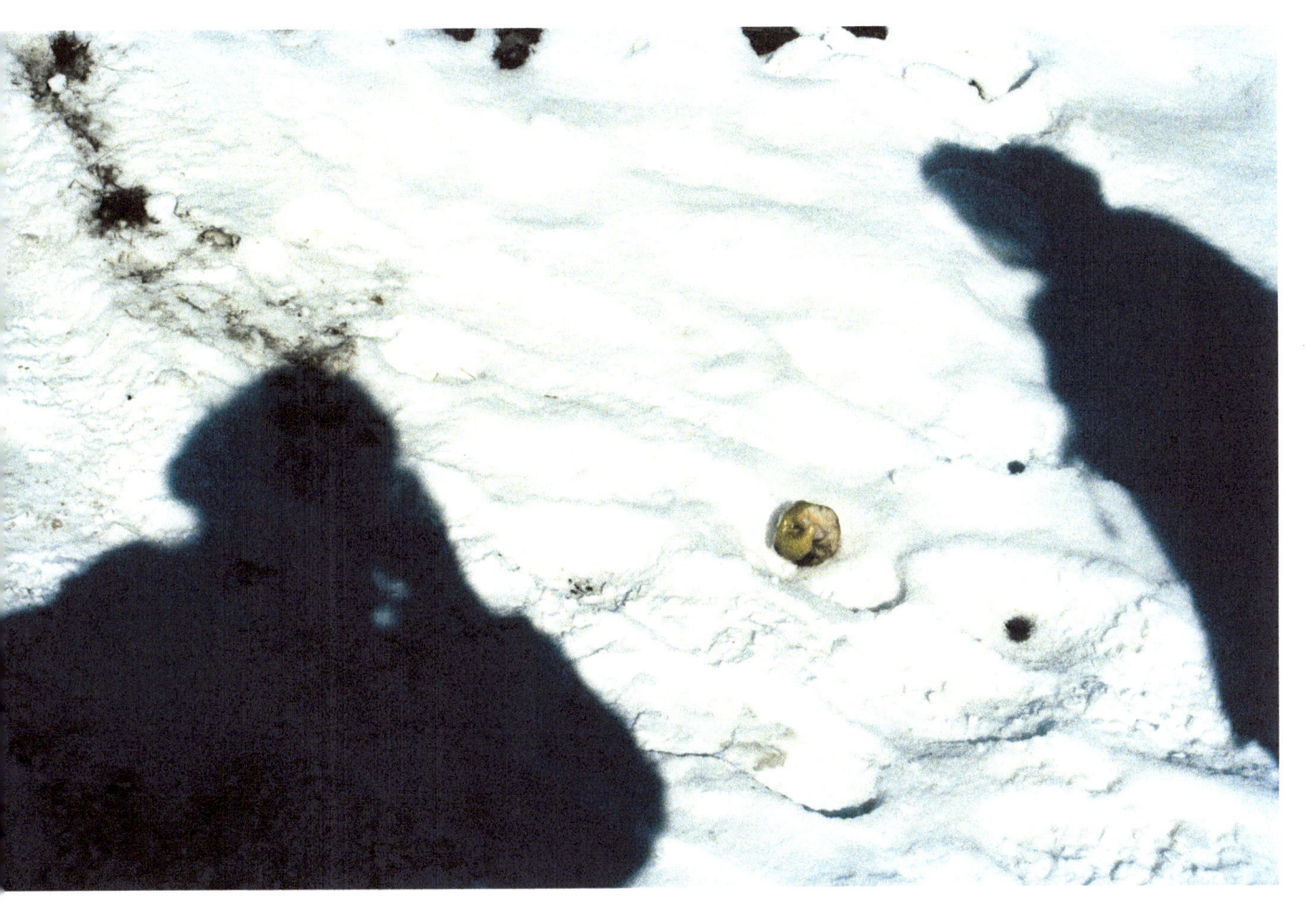

#23 3/6/14 12:06 pm Rochester, NY

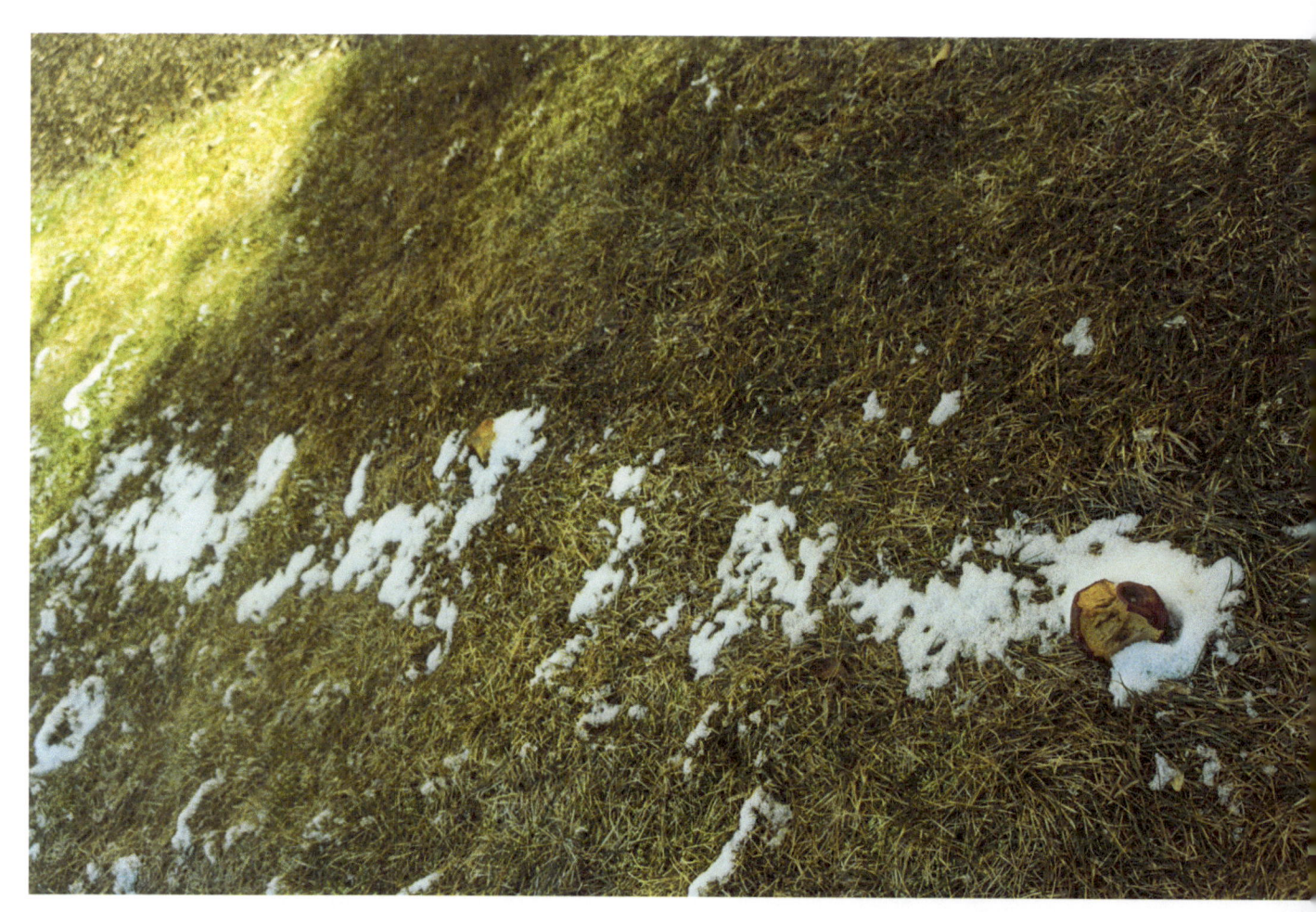

#24 3/6/14 12:12 pm Rochester, NY

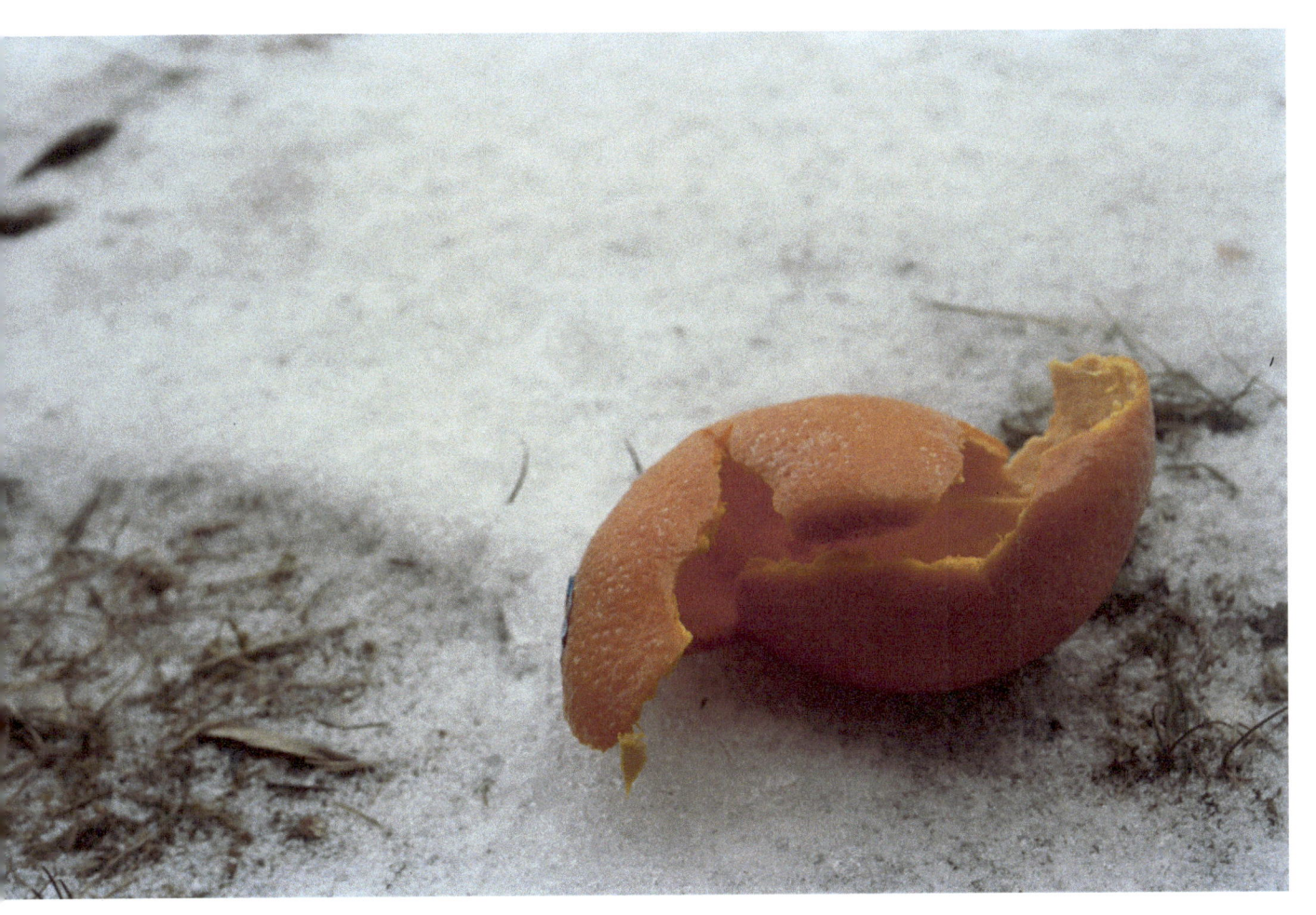

#25 3/9/14 12:47 pm Rochester, NY

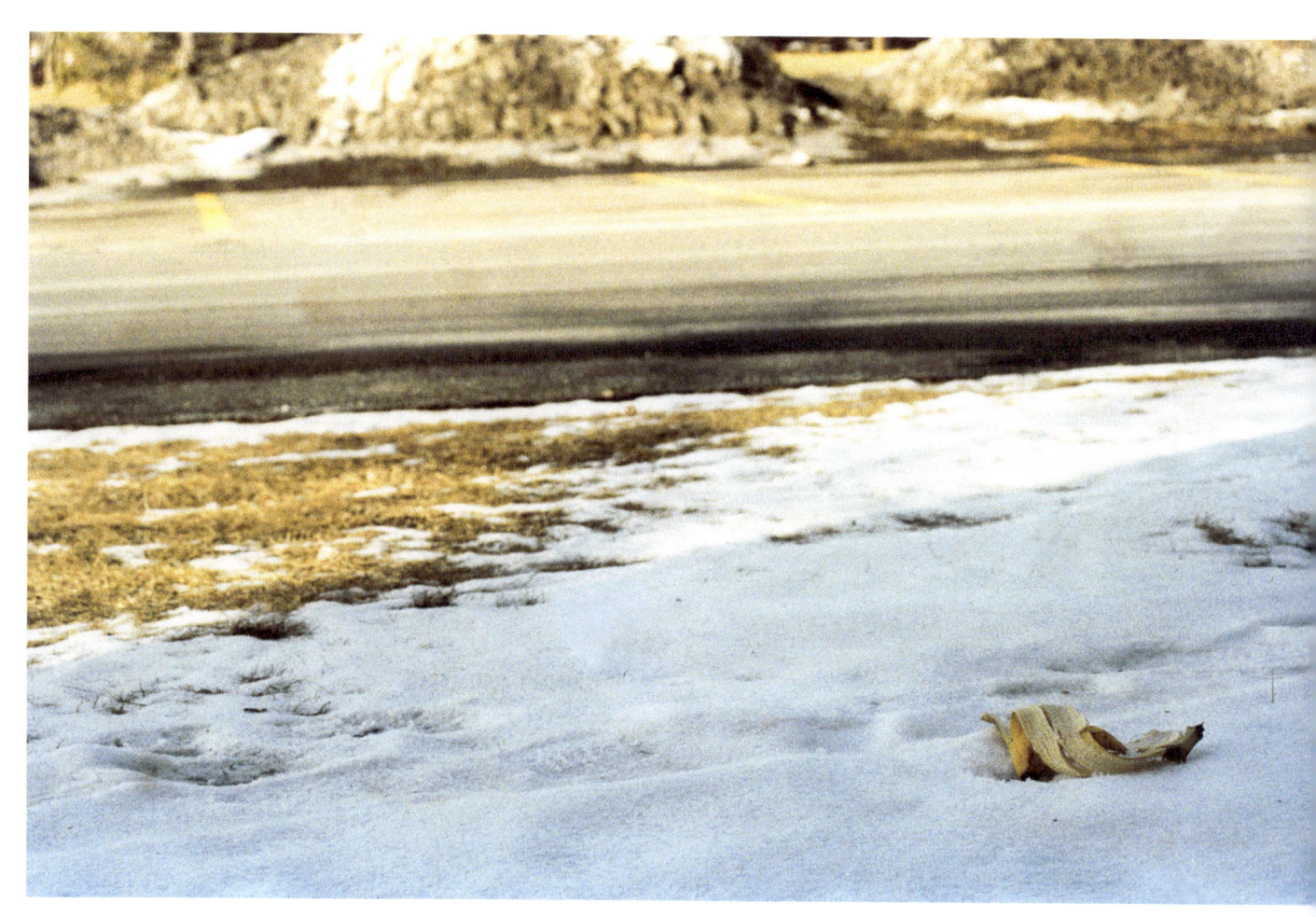

#26 3/9/14 4:14 pm Rochester, NY

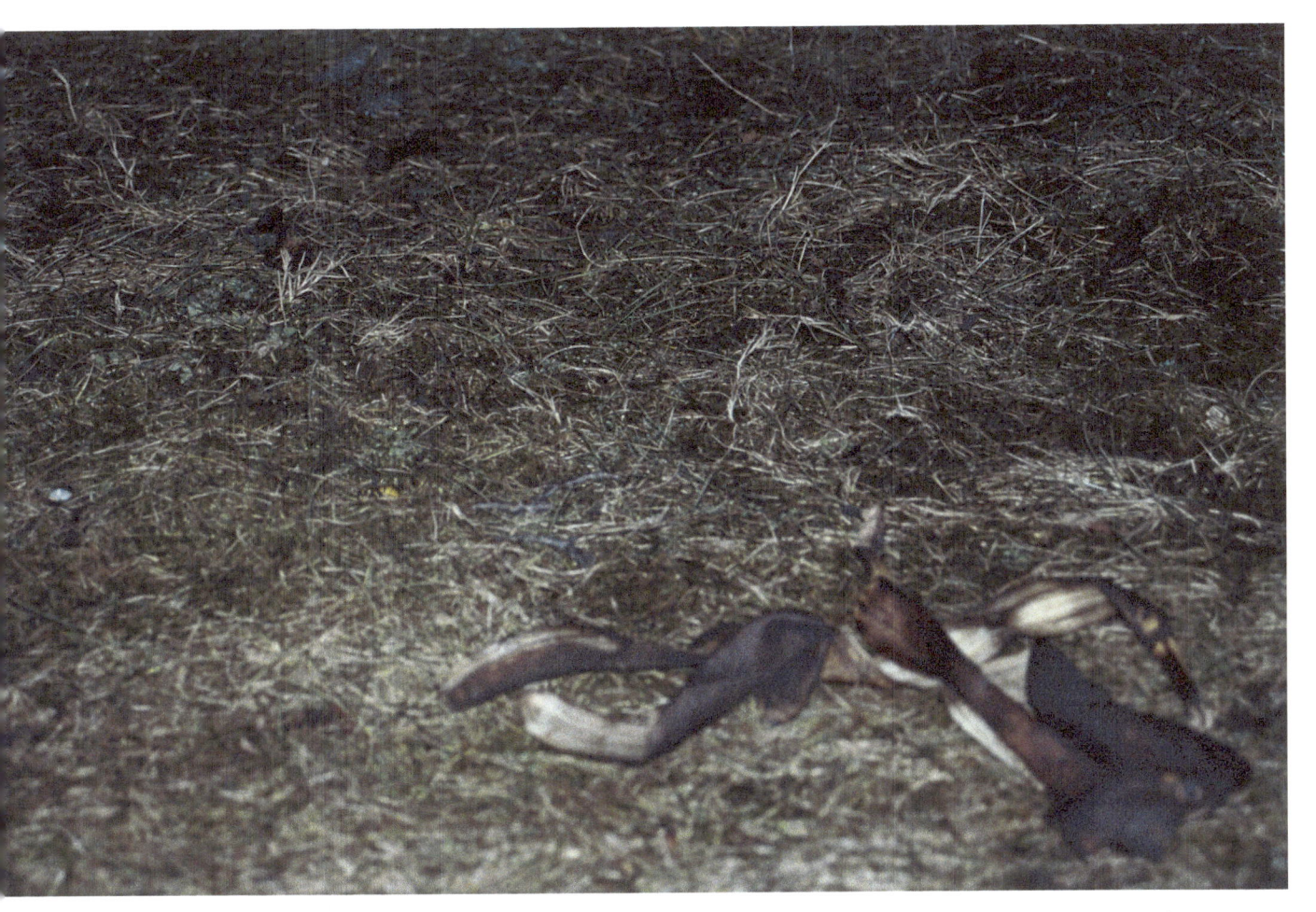

#27 3/11/14 10:13 pm Rochester, NY

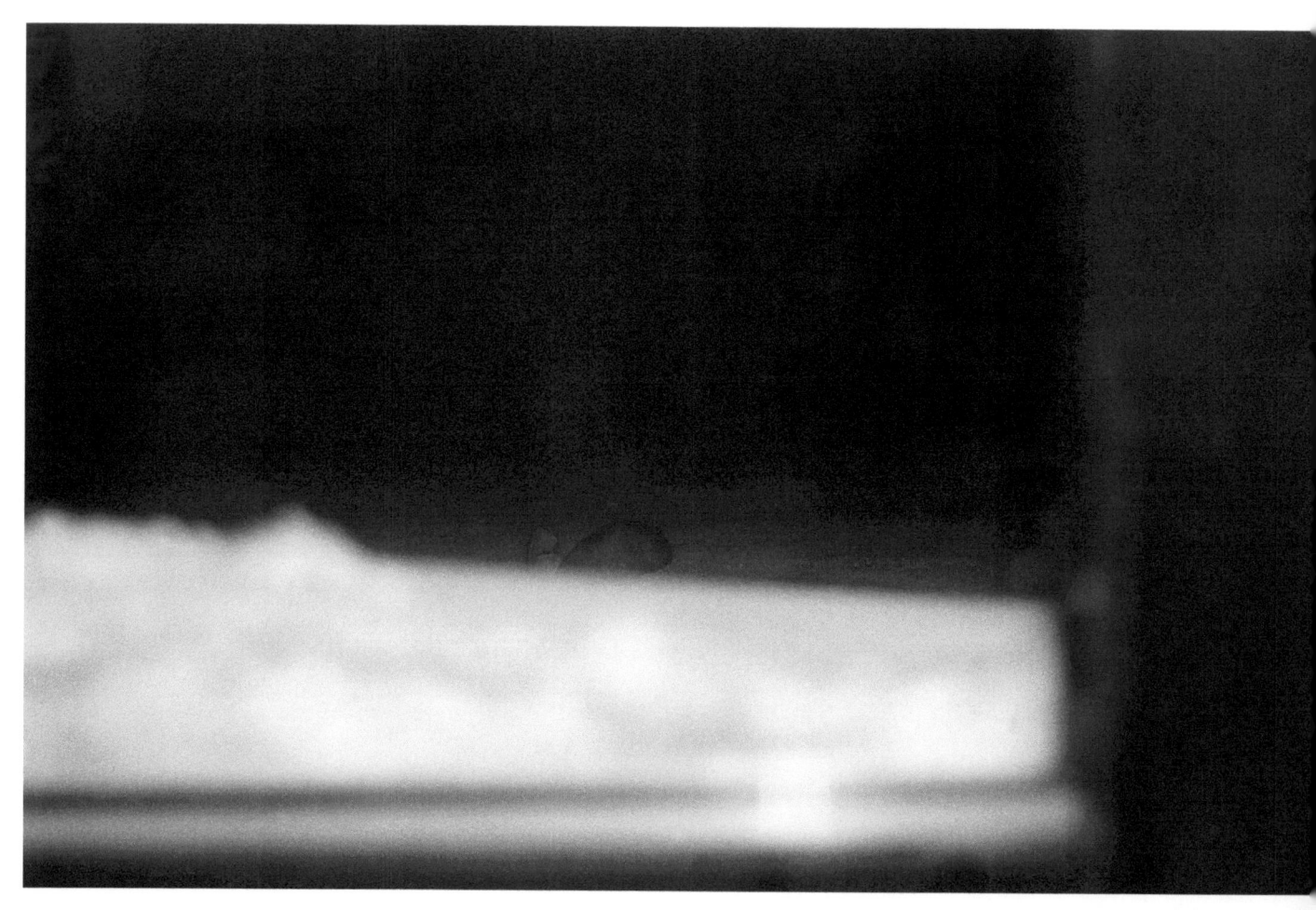

#28 3/13/14 8:11 pm Rochester, NY

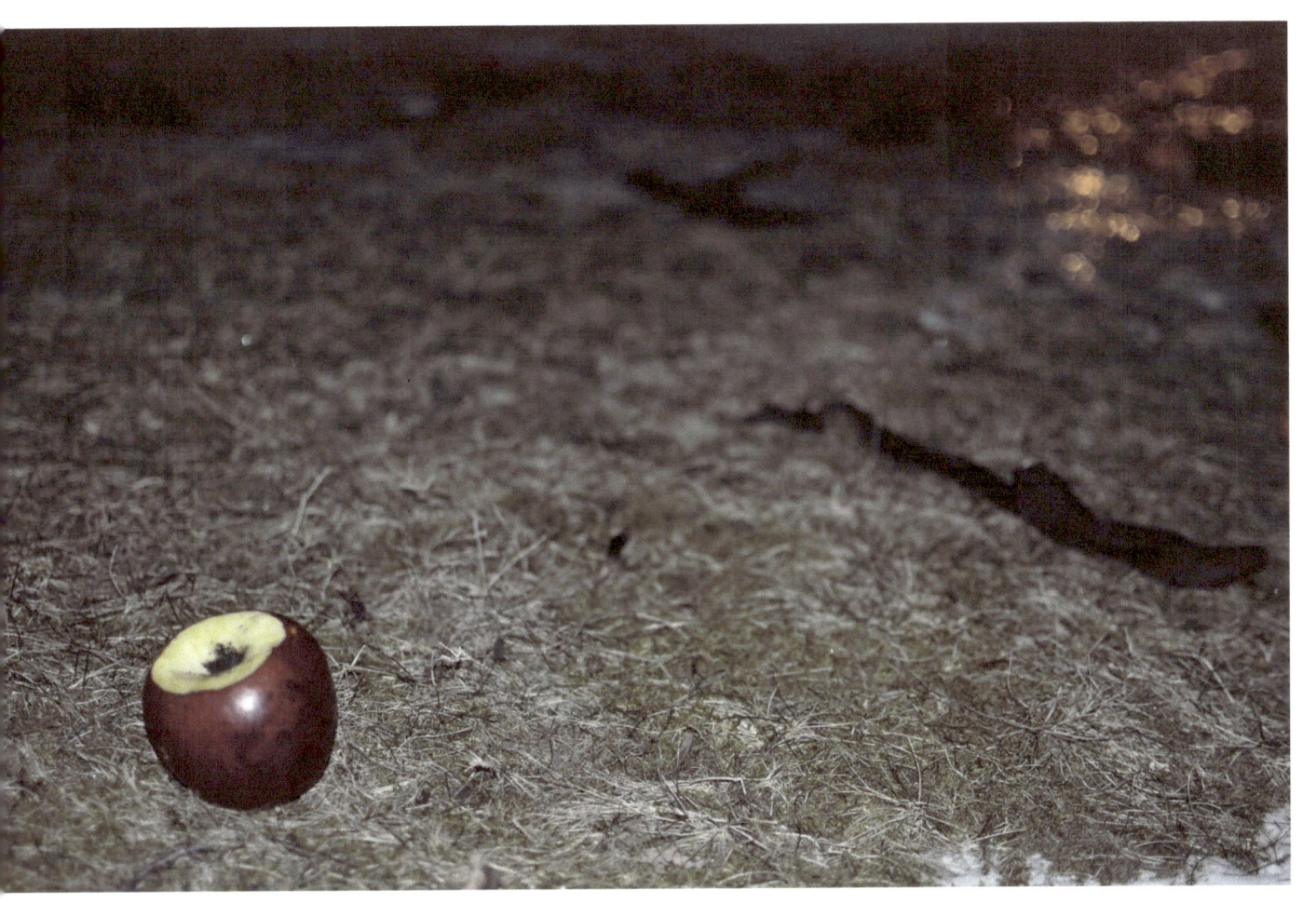

#29 3/16/14 11:25 pm Rochester, NY

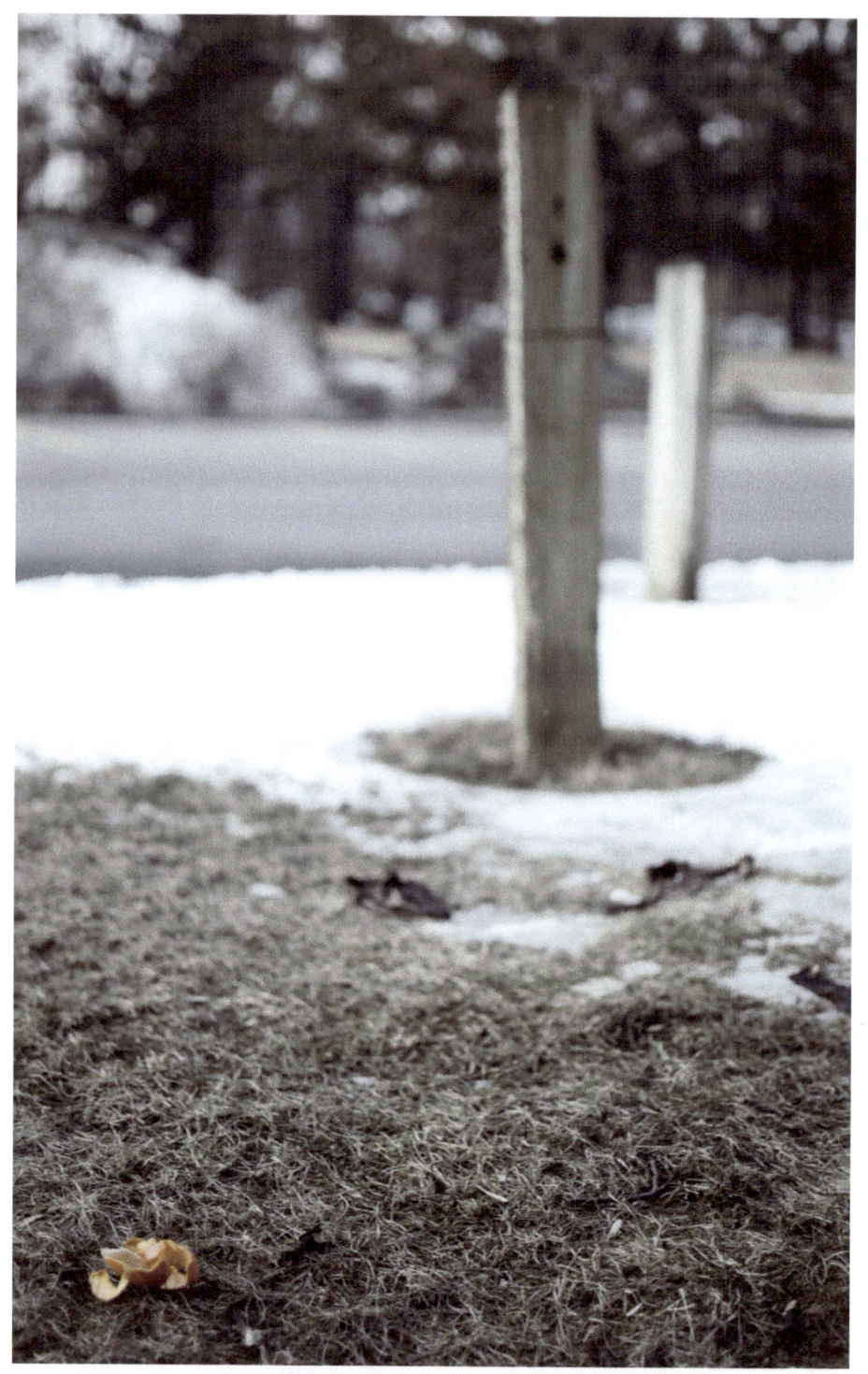

#30 3/17/14 7:27 pm Rochester, NY

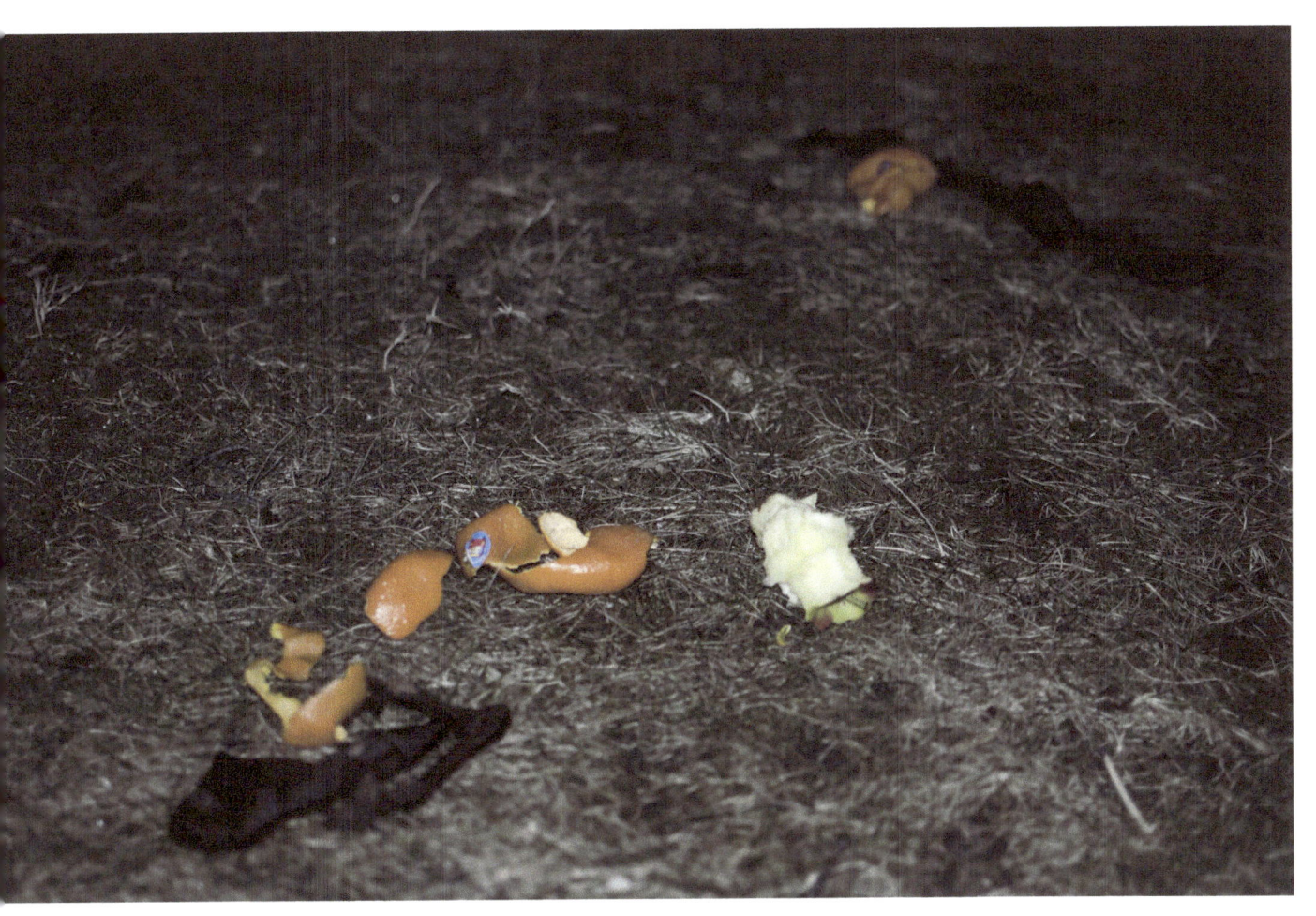

#31 3/20/14 9:36 pm Rochester, NY

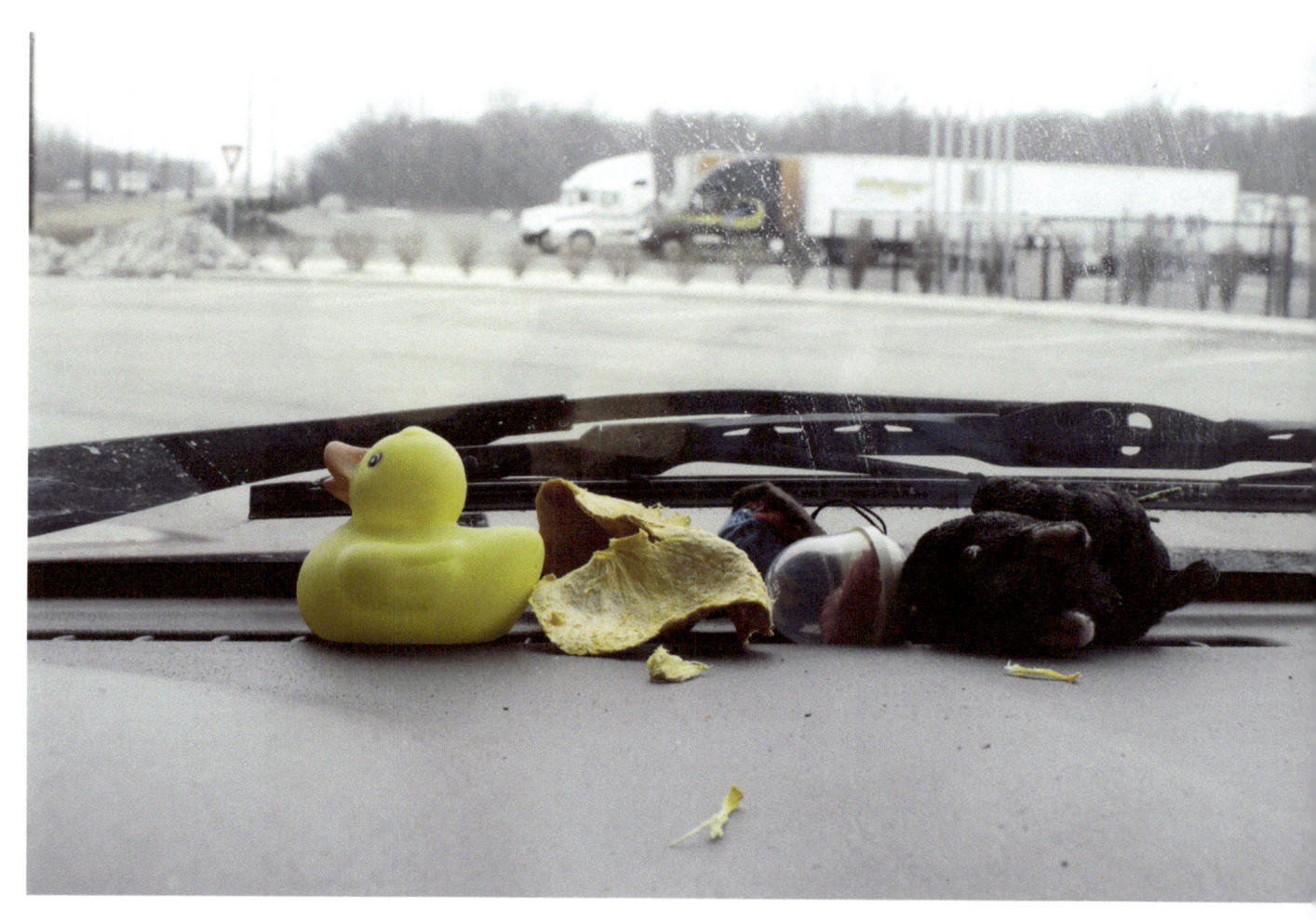

#32 3/22/14 1:45 pm Ohio

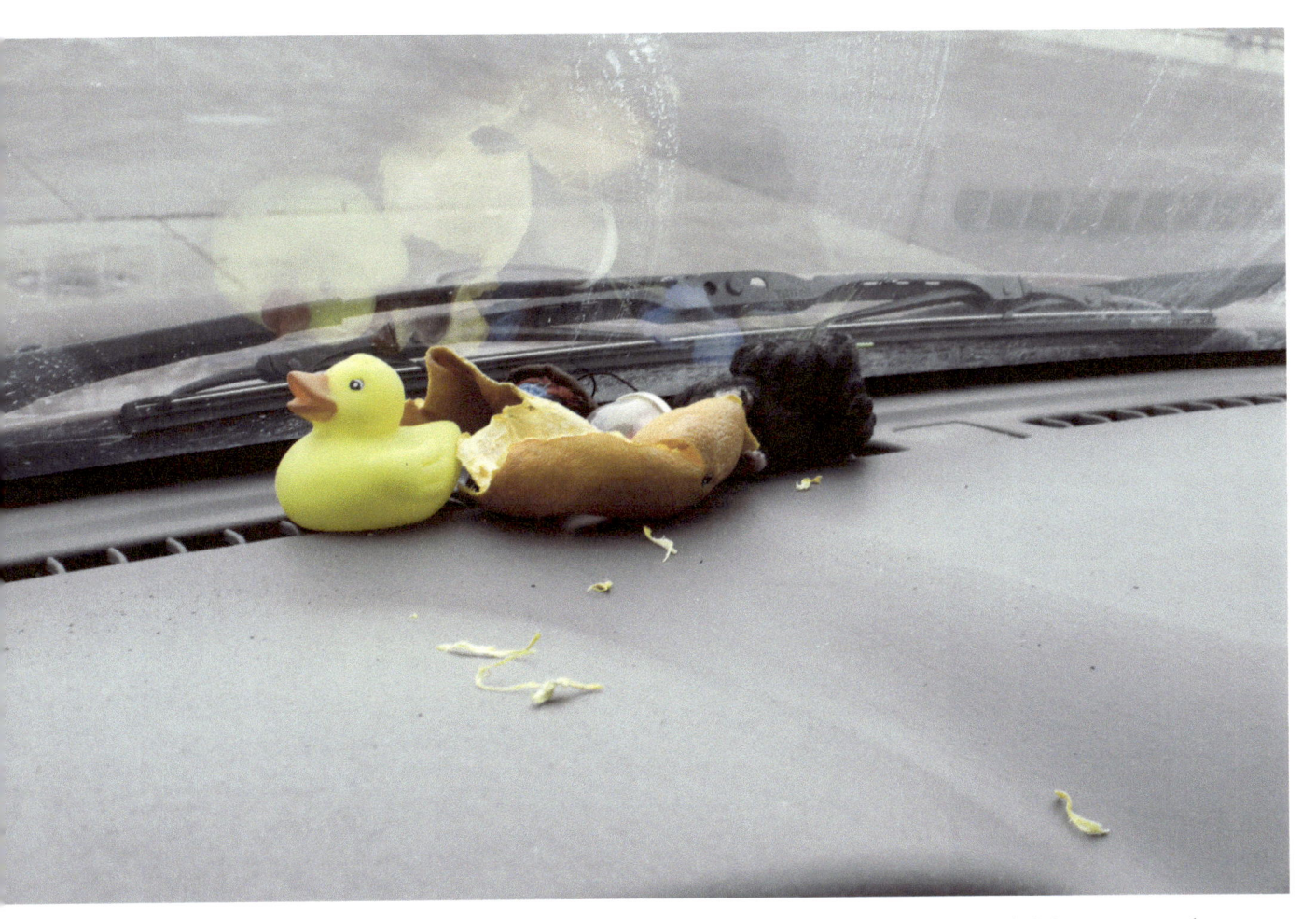

#33 3/22/14 4:22 pm Indiana

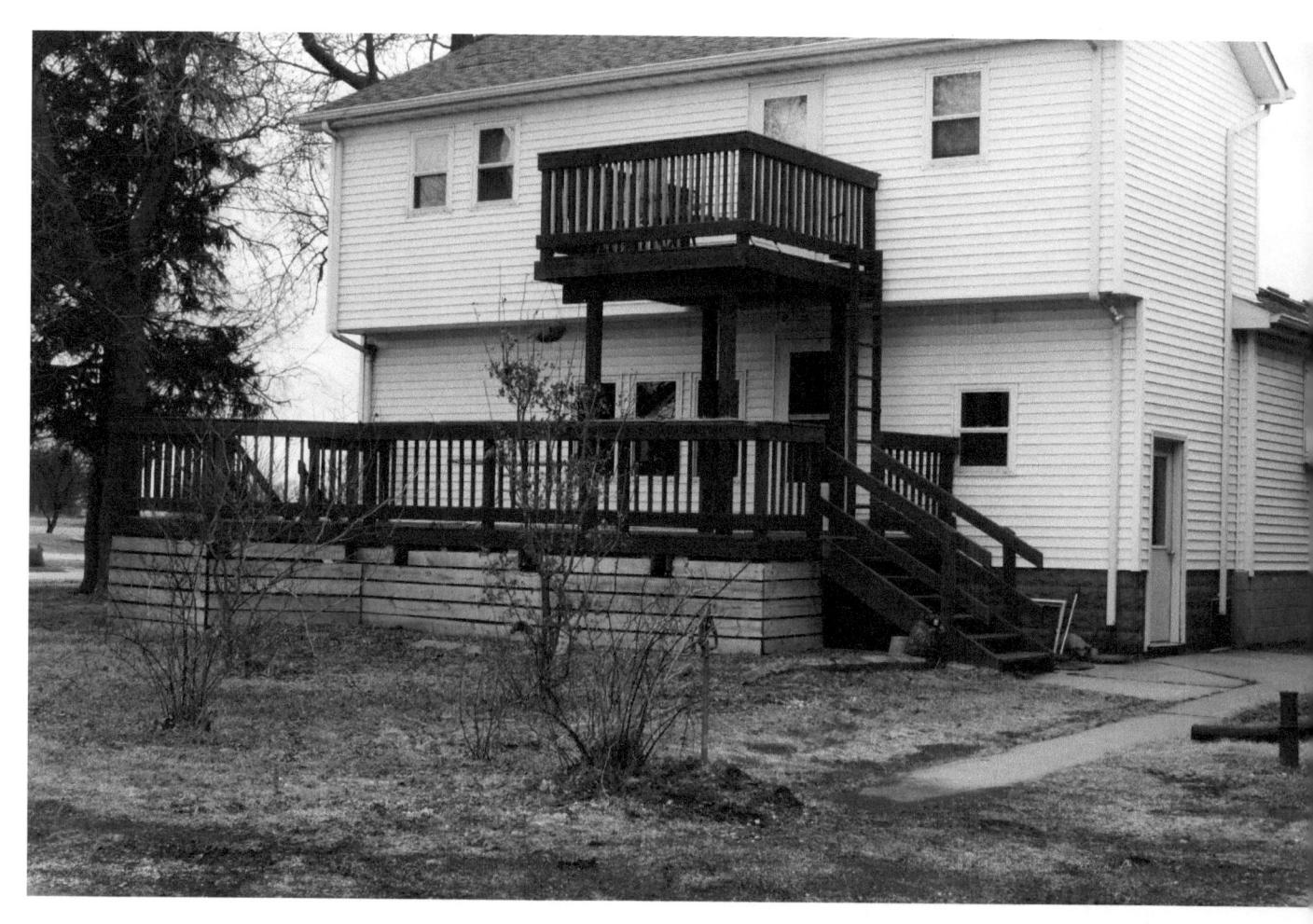

#34 3/22/14 5:05 pm Bonfield, IL

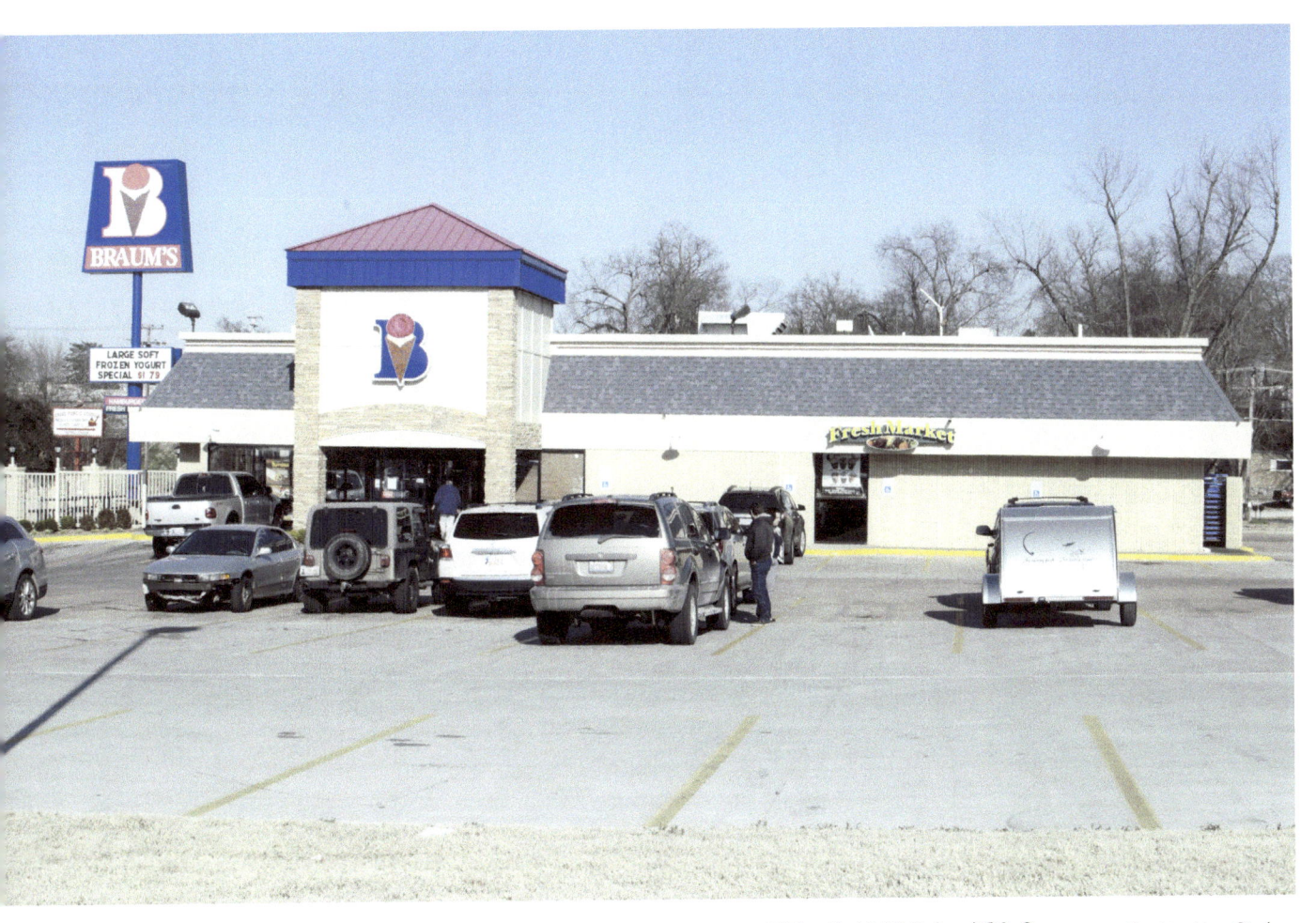

#35 3/25/14 5:20 pm Grove, OK

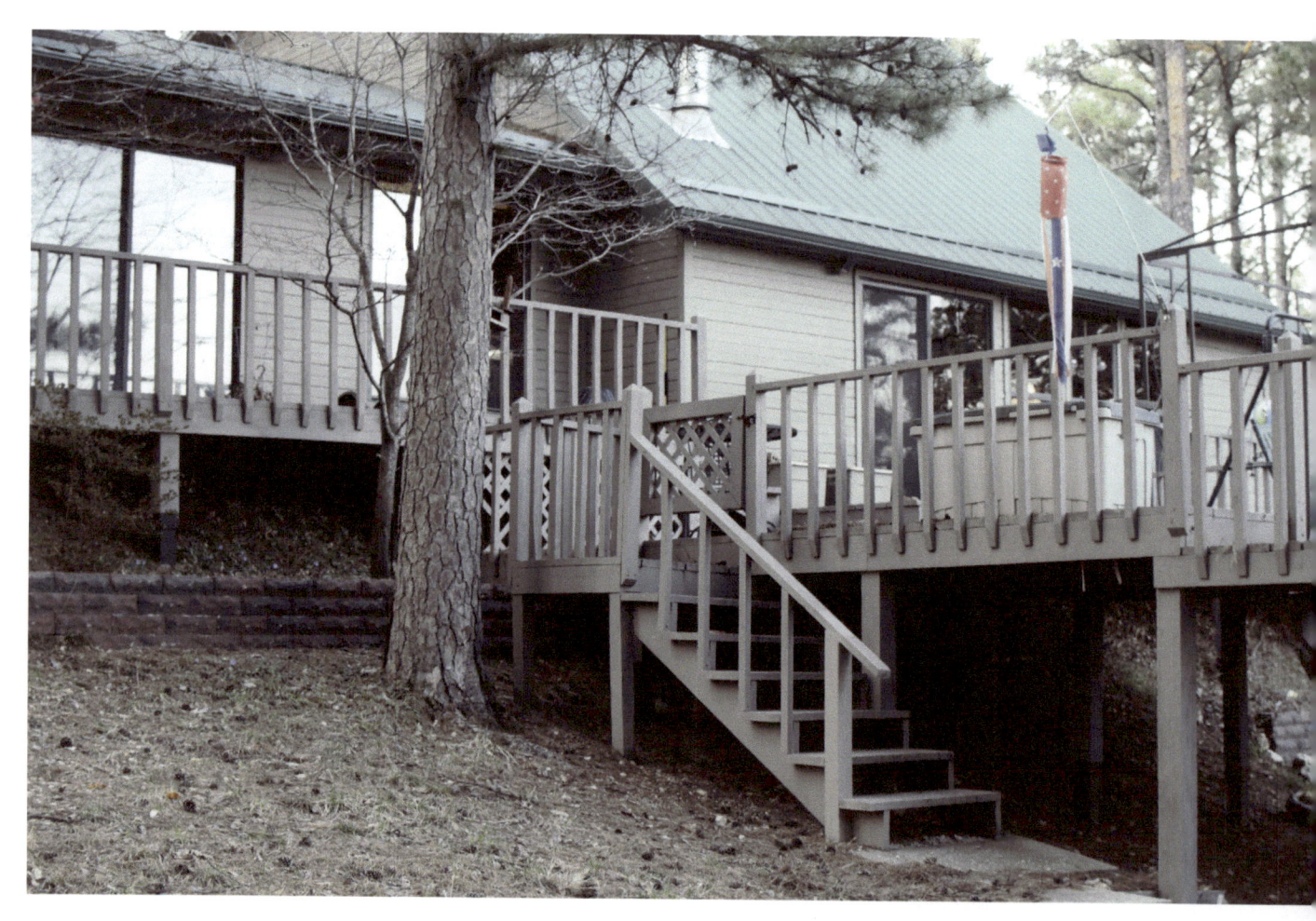

#36 3/25/14 8:24 pm Jay, OK

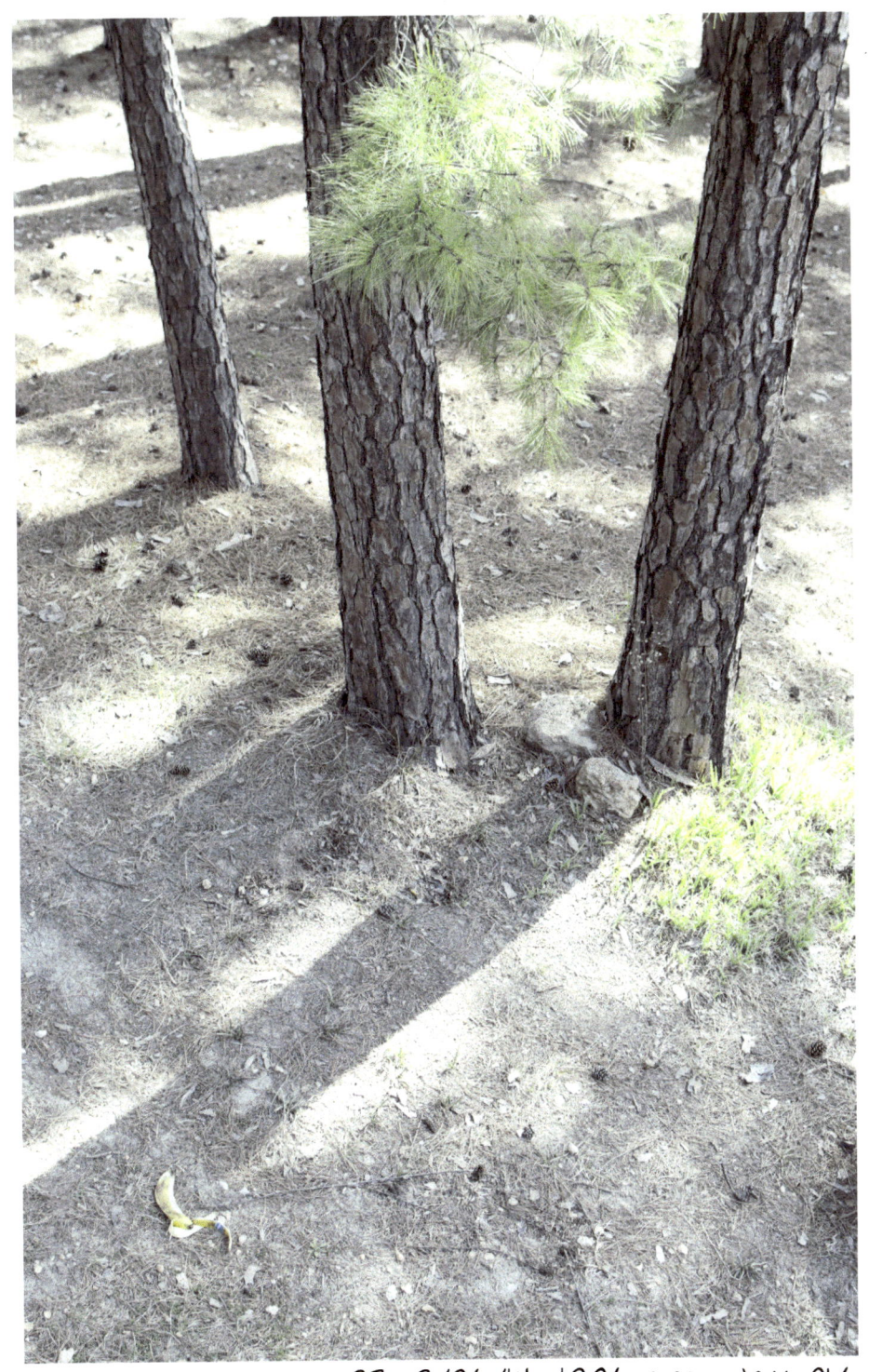

#37 3/26/14 10:26 am Jay, OK

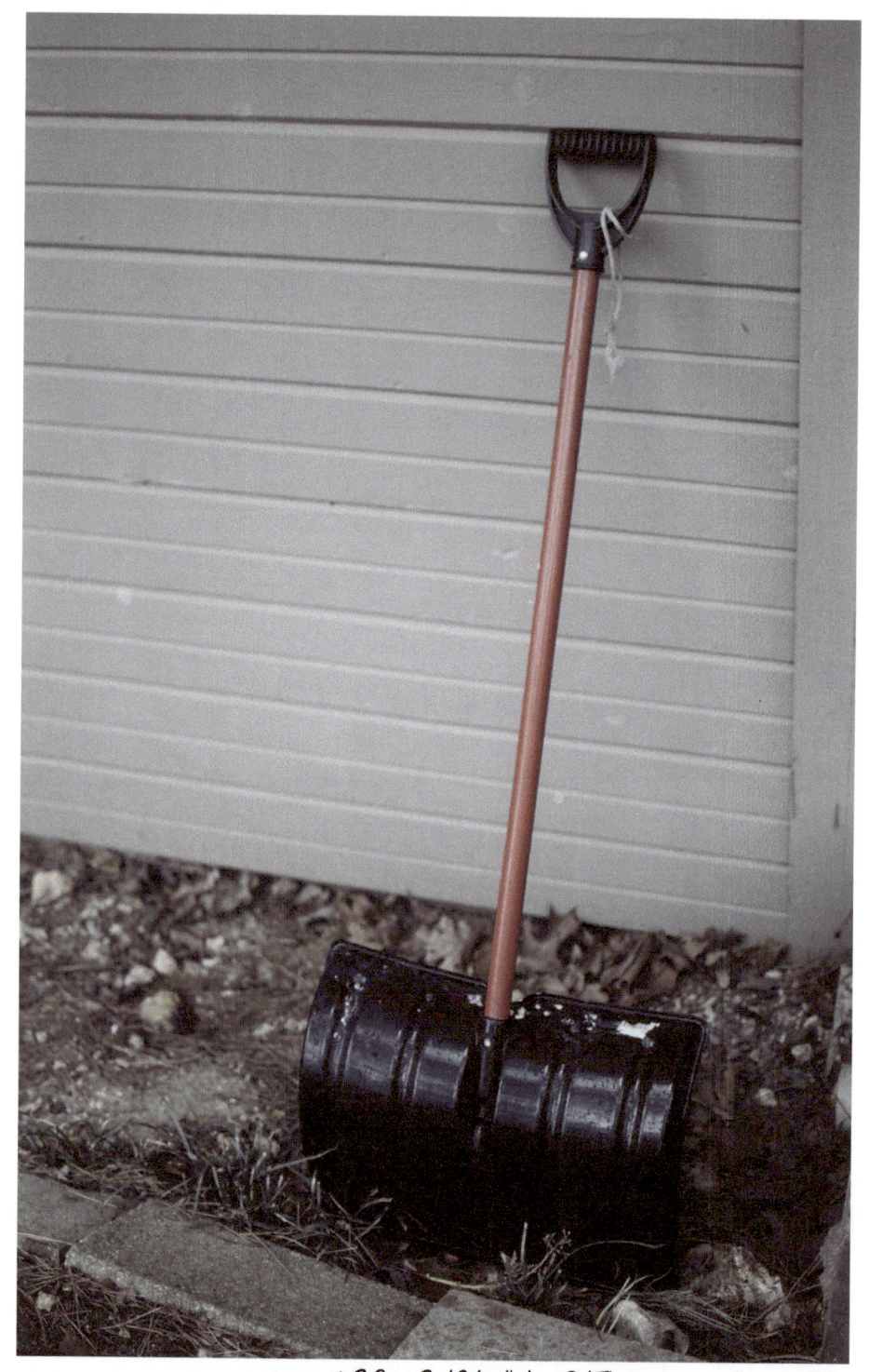

#38 3/26/14 3:56 pm Jay, OK

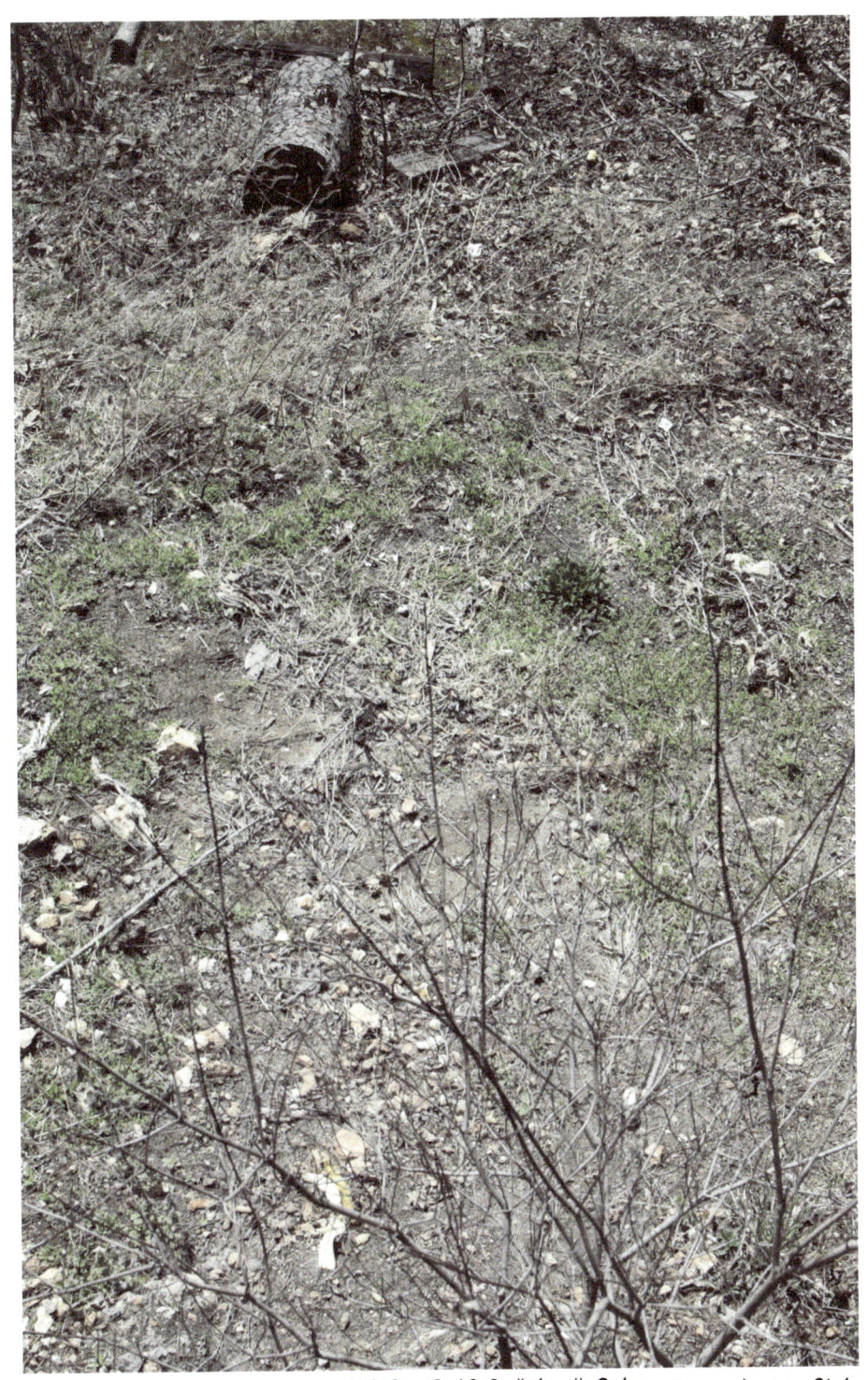

#39 3/28/14 11:04 am Jay, OK

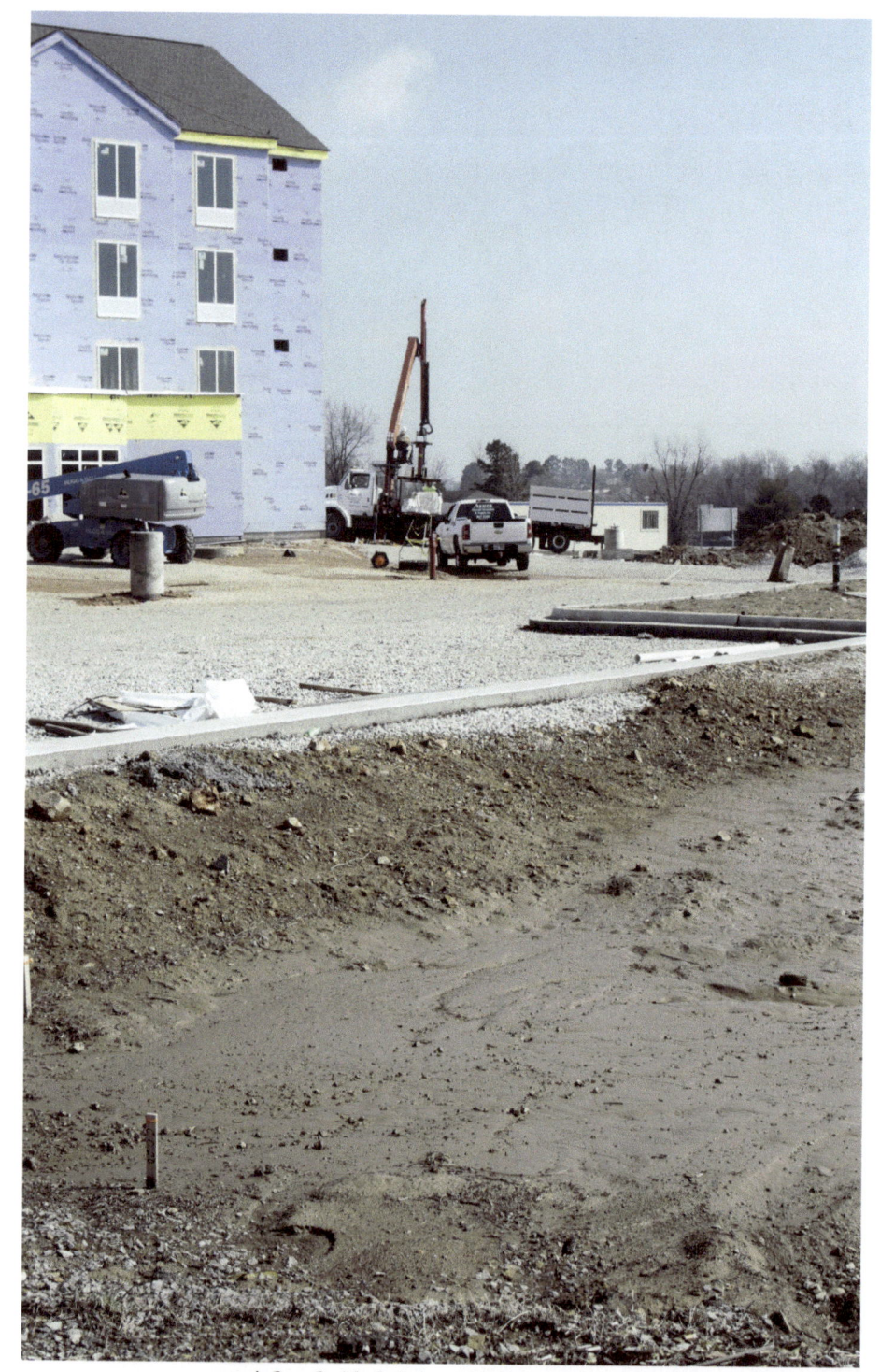

#40 3/29/14 10:41 am Fayetteville, AR

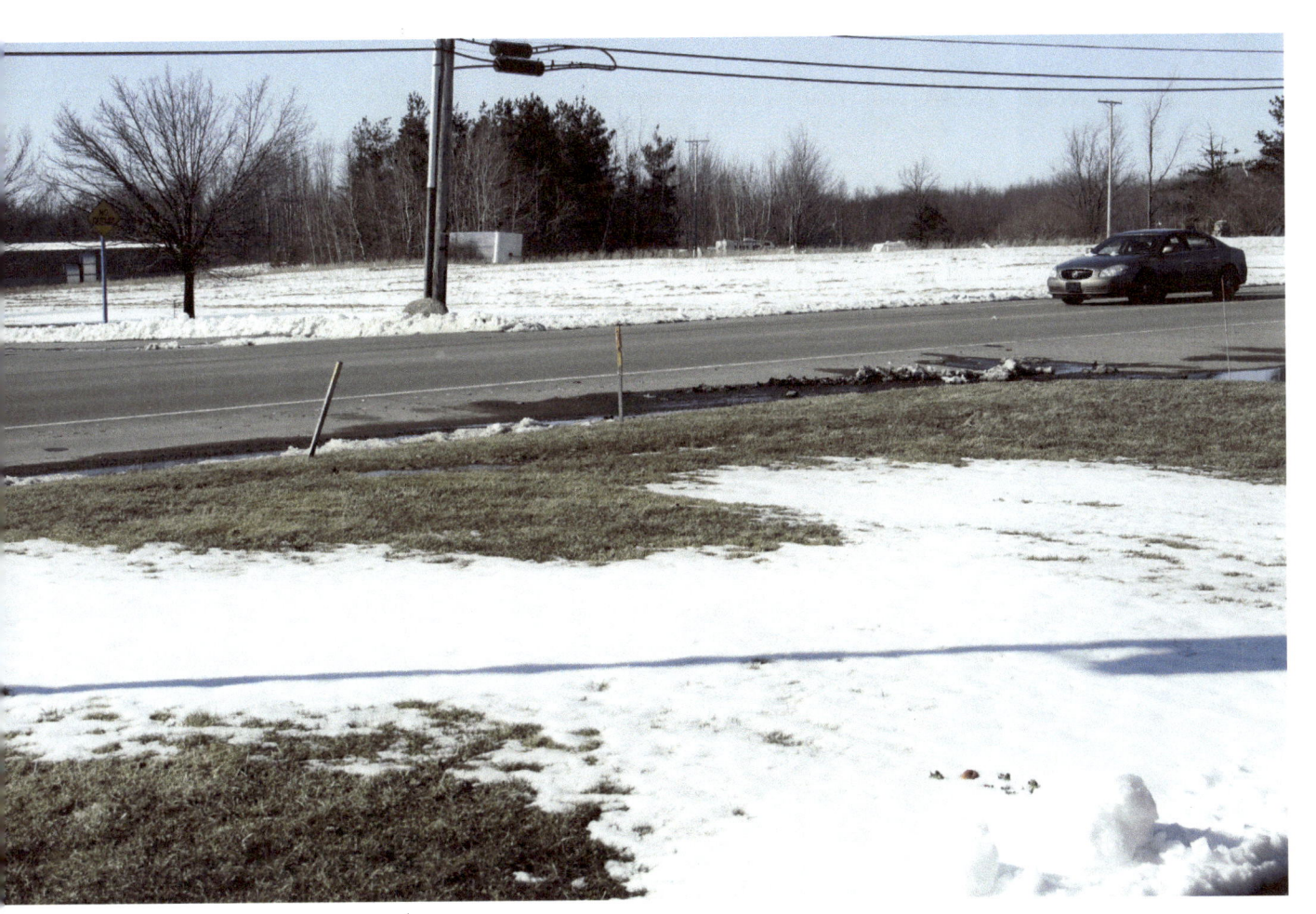

#41 3/30/14 4:49 pm Pennsylvania

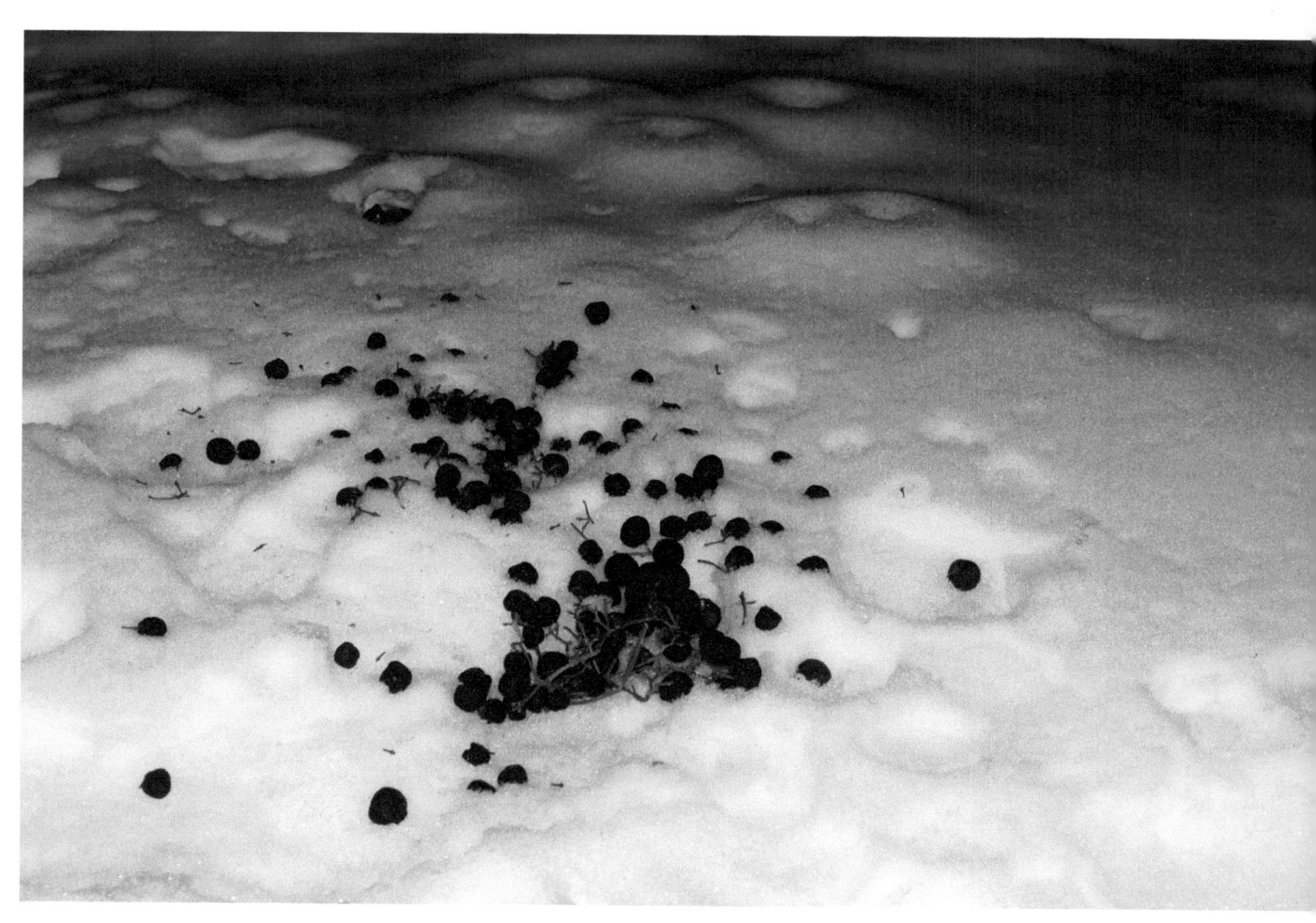

#42 3/30/14 8:18 pm Rochester, NY

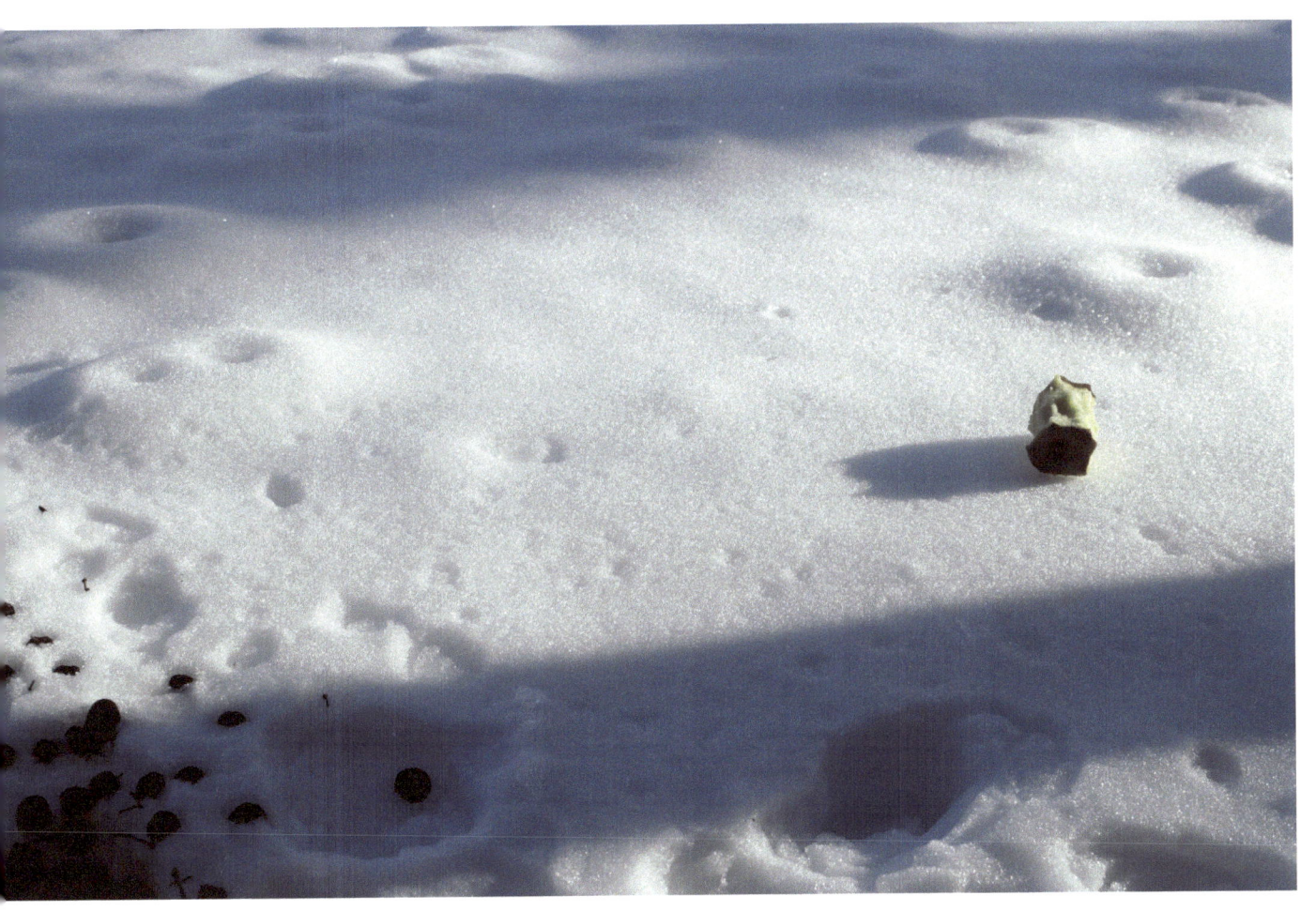

#43 3/31/14 8:24 am Rochester, NY

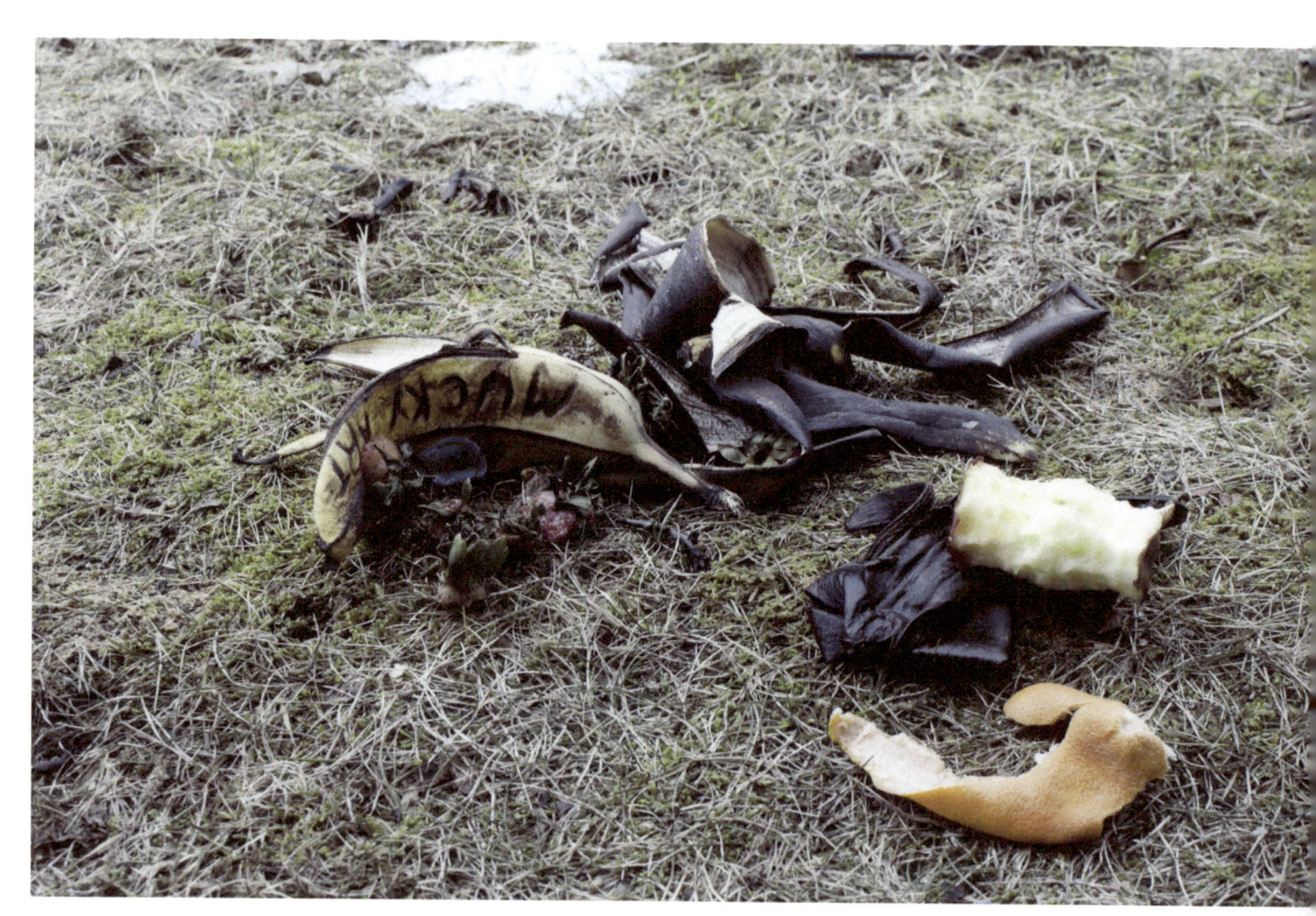

#44 4/4/14 6:16 pm Rochester, NY

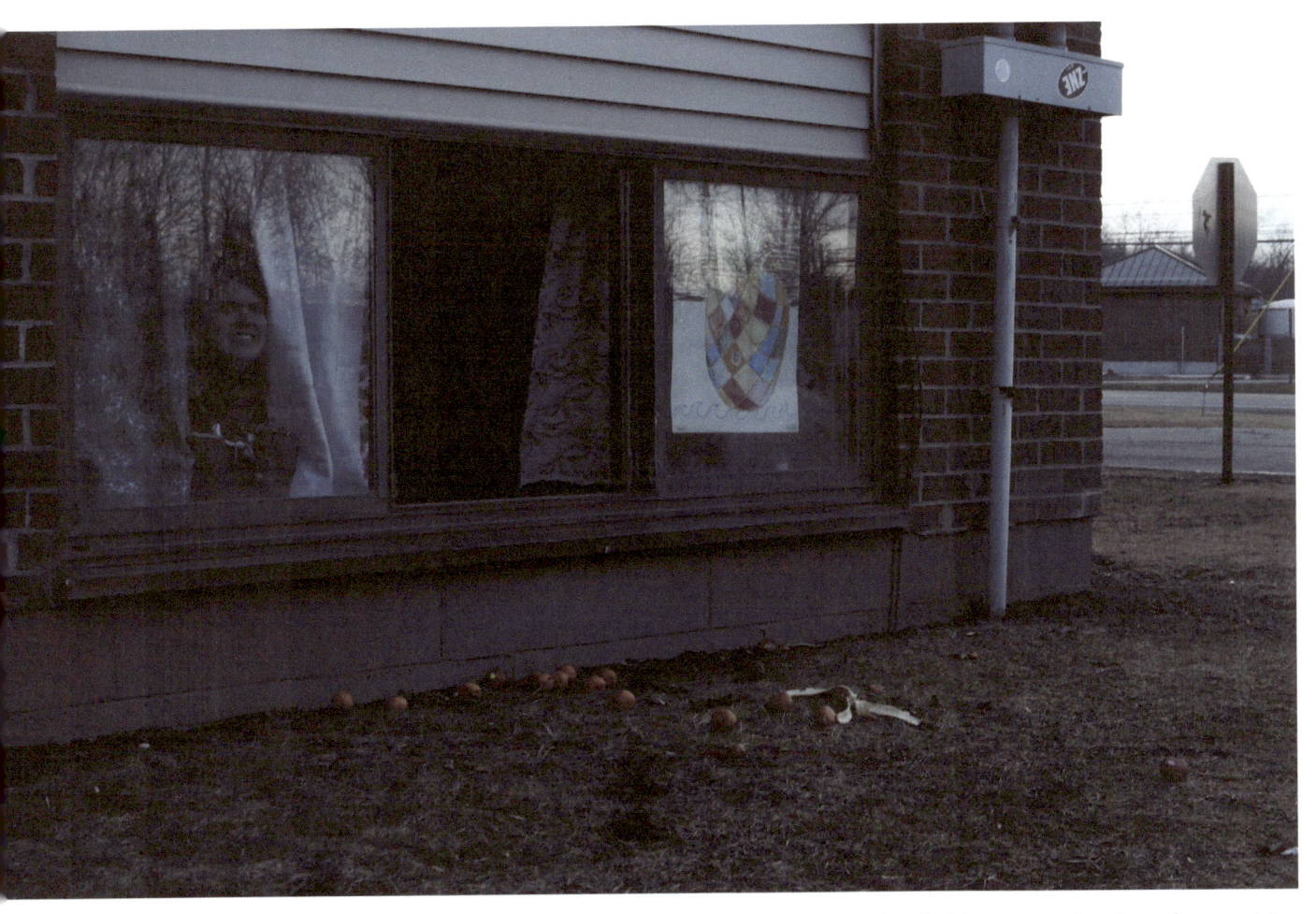

#45 4/6/14 7:36 pm Rochester, NY

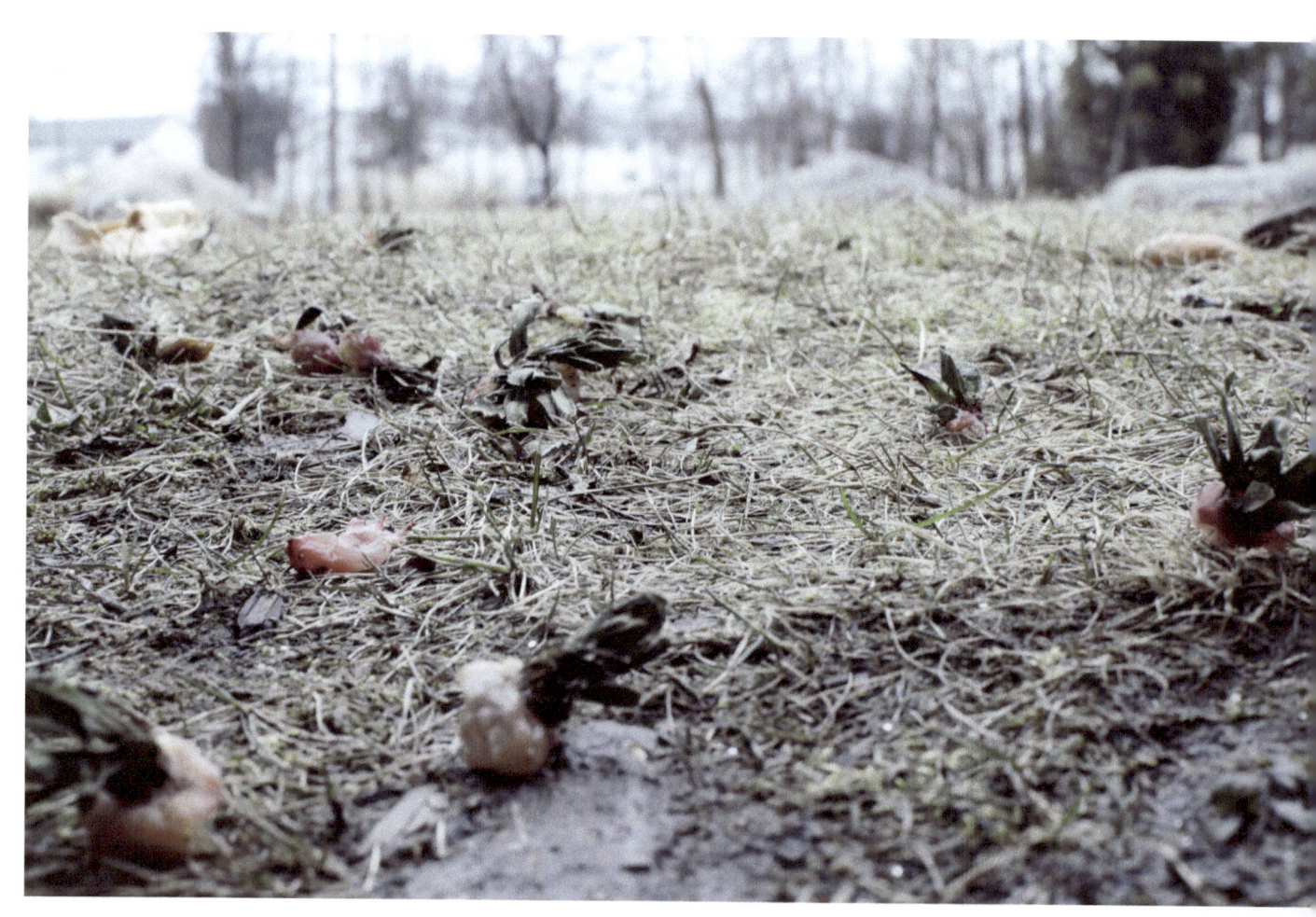

#46 4/7/14 4:11 pm Rochester, NY

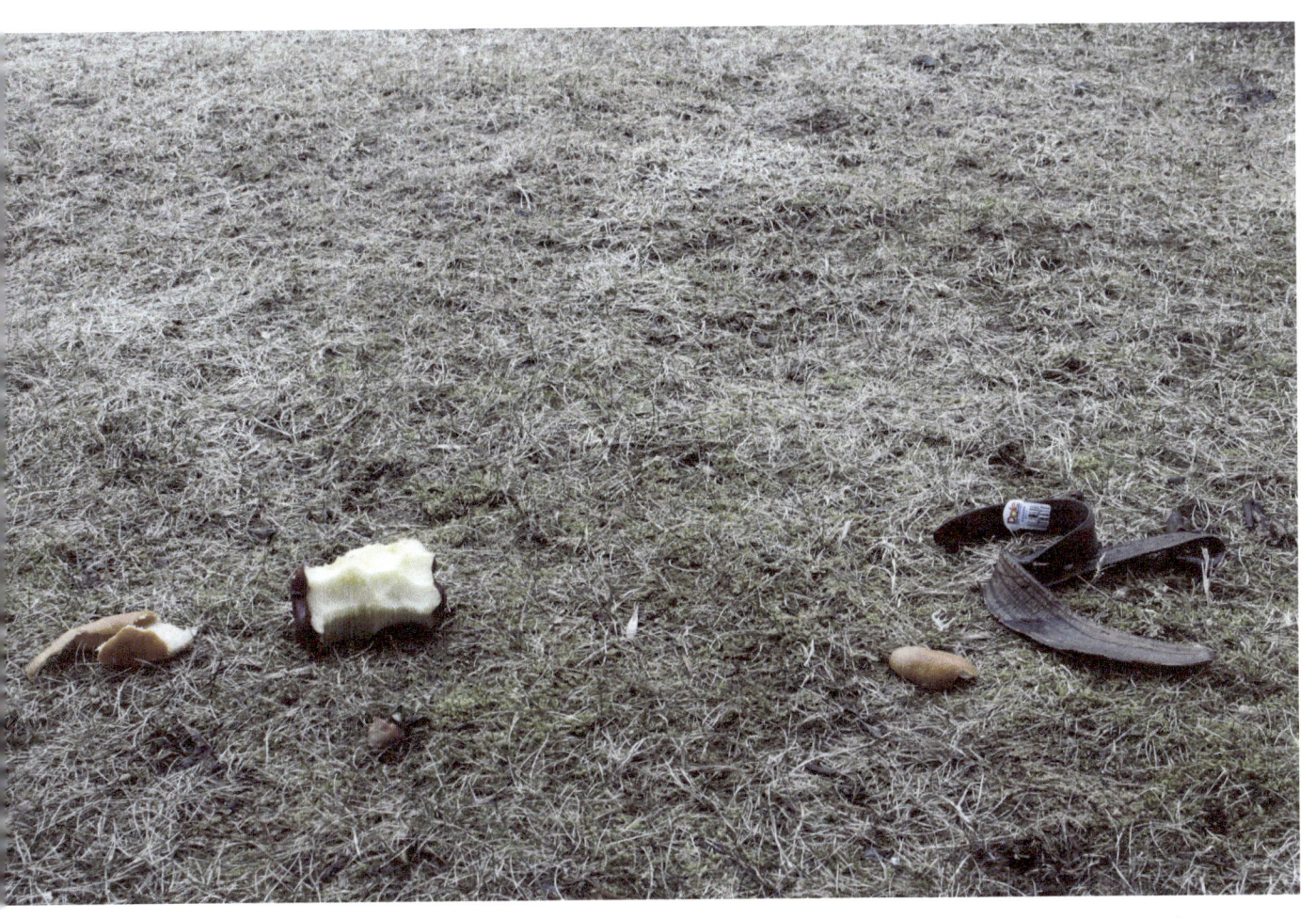

#47 4/8/14 4:14 pm Rochester, NY

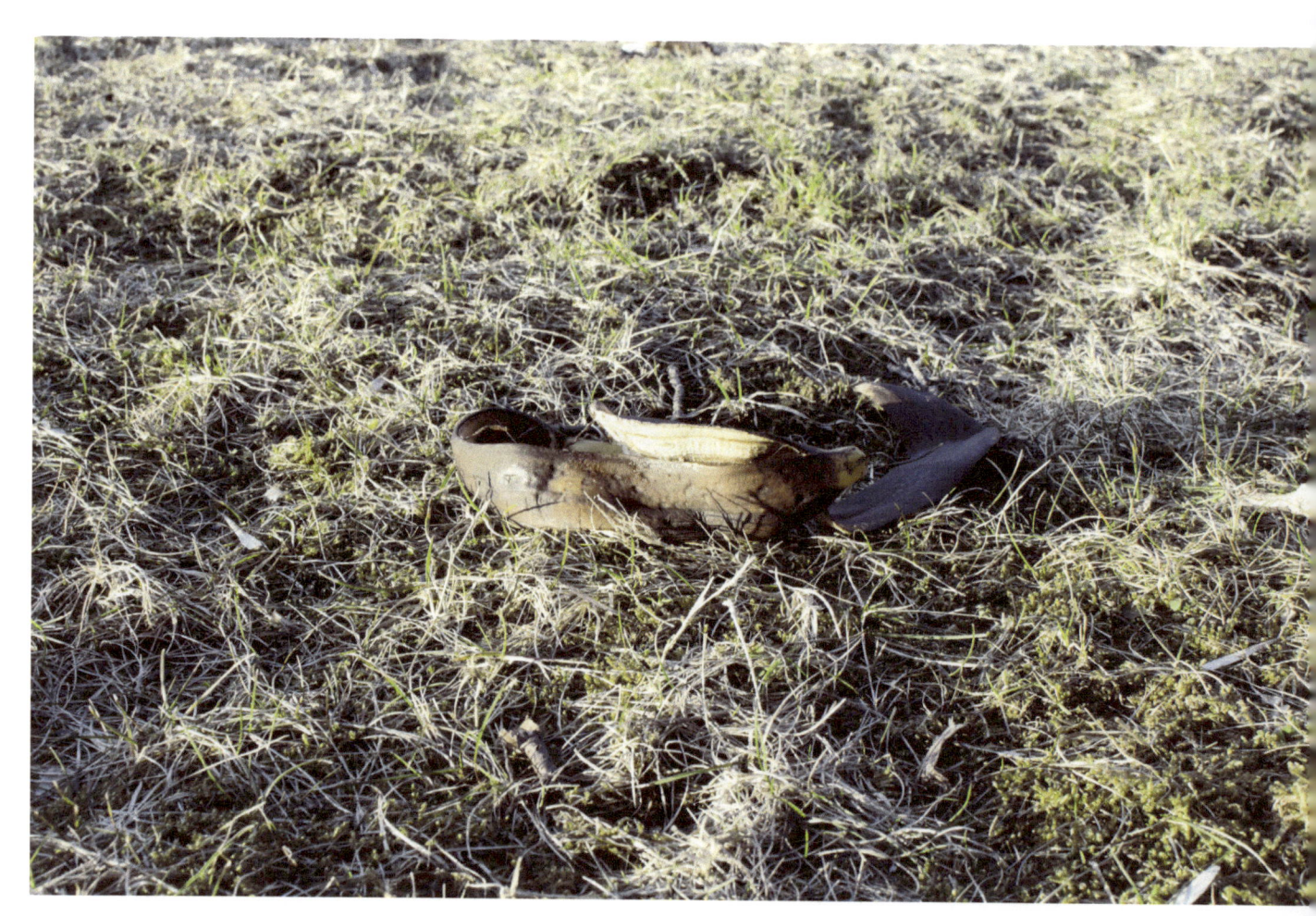

#48 4/9/14 7:09 pm Rochester, NY

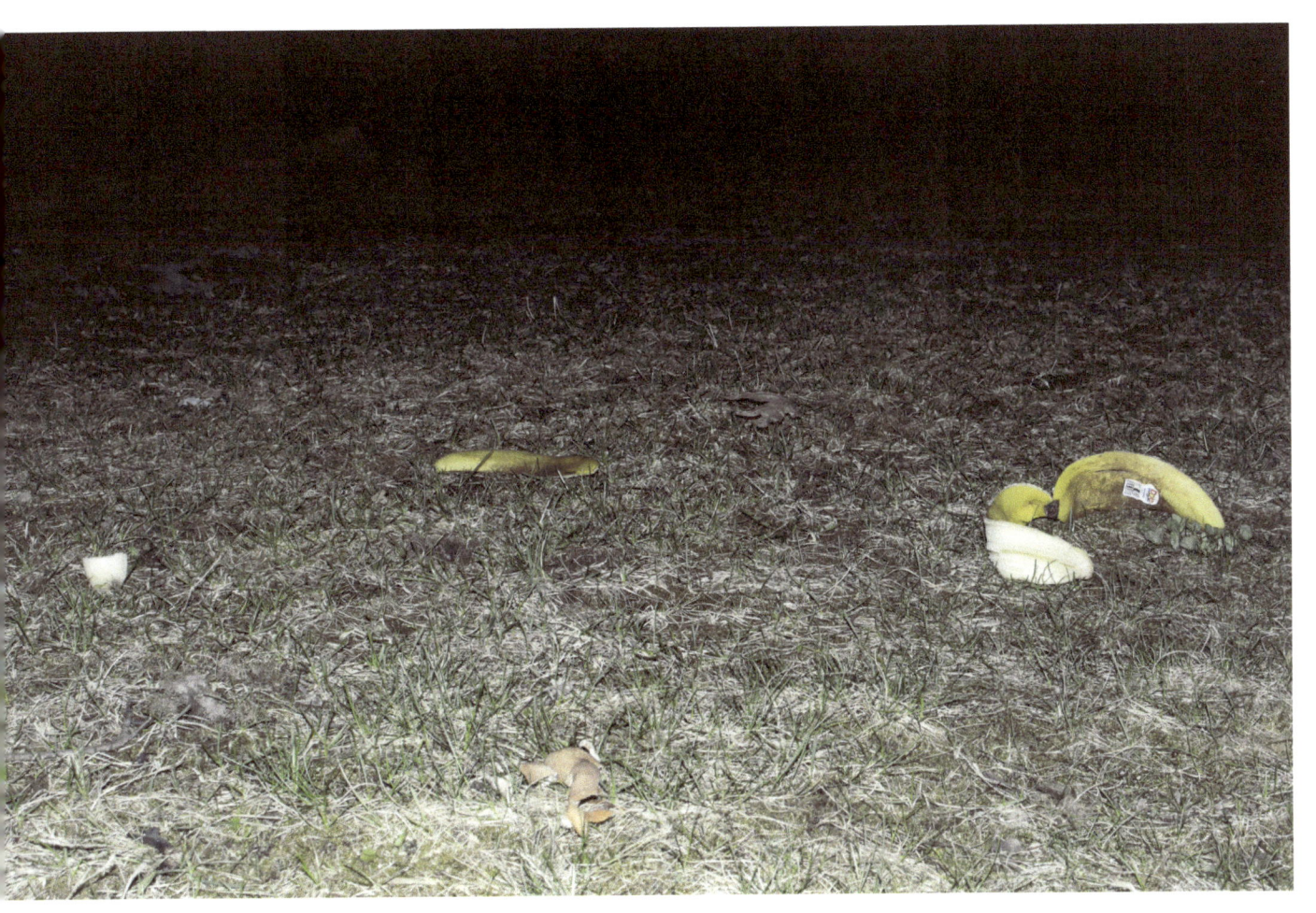

#49 4/28/14 9:50 pm Rochester, NY

www.ingramcontent.com/pod-product-compliance
Lightning Source LLC
Chambersburg PA
CBHW050900180526
45159CB00007B/2736